SPIRITUAL WARFARE
IN THE
21st CENTURY

To Char,
my friend for life!
Love you,
Blessings,
Dr. Judy

SPIRITUAL WARFARE
IN THE
21st CENTURY

*The
Re-emergence
of the
Deliverance
Ministry*

JUDITH LAWSON PhD

Outskirts Press, Inc.
Denver, Colorado

Spiritual Warfare in the 21st Century
The Re-emergence of the Deliverance Ministry
All Rights Reserved.
Copyright © 2011 Judith Lawson PhD
v3.0

Outskirts Press, Inc.
http://www.outskirtspress.com

ISBN: 978-1-4327-6731-0

Outskirts Press and the "OP" logo are trademarks belonging to Outskirts Press, Inc.

PRINTED IN THE UNITED STATES OF AMERICA

To be a Christian is to be a spiritual warrior. To engage in spiritual warfare is to walk consistently and victoriously through life with the Lord Jesus Christ. This book will teach you how to handle the weapons of that warfare effectively and obtain the victory.

Contents

Introduction

During the "Jesus Movement" of the 1960's and 1970's, ministries began to develop that came to be recognized as "deliverance ministries" or "spiritual warfare ministries" in which evil spirits were discerned and cast out of the lives of suffering individuals. Although this Jesus Movement was considered by some to be a "countercultural phenomenon" it had in it a spiritual revival aspect that no one can deny. Many were saved, filled with the Holy Spirit with the evidence of speaking in tongues. Many others were delivered from demonic oppression and healed of various diseases, disorders and dysfunctions.

However, there were others in the Body of Christ, equally sincere, who raised serious questions about the movement's validity. Unfortunately these differences of opinion led to a polarizing effect, with those holding to Cessationism, (the belief that the supernatural gifts of the apostolic church ceased with the death of John, the last Apostle) strongly contending that the Christian believer's power to get healed and delivered from evil spirits was established once and for all at the point of salvation.

Regrettably these deliverance and healing ministries faded into oblivion and have remained there for three to four decades. However, the signs are clearly before us that we are today living in the closing days of this earth's history and that this warfare is intensifying to an unprecedented degree as this conflict draws to a close. In these last days, it is becoming obvious that learning how to combat demonic oppression is crucial for the physical, spiritual, psychological, and emotional growth of the Christian and thank God, there is evidence that there has, indeed, been a re-emergence in the Church of the ministry of spiritual warfare in this, the 21st Century.

God's Word teaches us that as long as we are to remain upon the earth we will be engaged in spiritual warfare with the enemy of our souls, Satan. This book will explain how to use the weapons of that warfare. There are some who would prefer to ignore the devil with the false and dangerous idea that he will leave them alone. Many Christians believe the Devil's lies and are simply not interested in hearing about spiritual warfare and many pastors have succeeded in convincing their congregants that the devil is not a threat. Nothing could be further from the truth. The truth is, when we signed up to become Christians, we automatically entered into the arena of warfare, whether we like it or not.

We must be careful to not become obsessed with demon spirits, blaming demonic forces for every uncomfortable situation or flaw in one's character, but we must teach about spiritual warfare because demonic activity is a major reason why Christians remain ill, have so many diseases, die too early, and have so many perplexing problems in their lives. Sadly, spiritual warfare is a key ingredient that is sadly missing in the Church today.

It must be noted that heathen practices of *exorcism* are to be distinguished from Christian deliverance. Heathen exorcism is a magic defense, and belongs to the sphere of occultism (Koch 249).

It is true, Jesus defeated the enemy at Calvary; however, the mental acquiescence that Jesus defeated the devil and that we have authority over him is not enough. Many continually allow Satan, whom we know was defeated, to beat them down, torment, terrorize, and take advantage of them. They forget that they are not victims, but victors!

Although we might be strong believers in setting people free from demonic bondage, spiritual warfare should never be an end in itself, but a means to an end. As we strive to bring balance to this much-neglected ministry we must attempt to avoid either over emphasizing spiritual warfare, seeing demons everywhere, or under emphasizing it with the lie that any acknowledgement of Satan is an invitation for demonic activity.

Our victory over our enemy, Satan, has never been in question. What Christ did on the cross was for all time and for all people if they will accept it. We are not to fear the enemy but become knowledgeable about his activities. Military strategists involve their troops in learning even the minutest details about the enemy they will be facing. They go into battle well prepared and they know what to expect when they arrive on the battlefield. We can be certain that Satan knows us, his enemies, quite well and is continually arming himself with information about us in order to defeat us.

Spiritual warfare is constant. The war is being waged against us 24 hours a day, 7 days a week. Satan never calls in sick! He is relentless in his attempts to put a stop to and curtail the work of God in us and through us. In John 10:10 we are told,

"The thief (Satan) cometh not but for to steal, kill and to destroy; I (Jesus) am come that they might have life, and that they might have it more abundantly."Yes, God loves us and has a plan for each one of our lives. However, Satan hates us and has a plan for our lives as well.

God teaches us in Isaiah 5:13,

"My people are gone into captivity because they have no knowledge,"

and again in Hosea 4:6,

"My people are destroyed for lack of knowledge."

The ignorance of the believer is the devil's only real power. It is the only way that a child of God can be destroyed.

Sin is the main reason evil spirits have been given a legal right to enter a life to torment and harass, but it should be understood that there are other reasons as well. In some instances a legal right may have been given to the enemy by the sins of the parents or by former generations, accidents, traumatic experiences, abuse, or the actions of other people. The devil is a great opportunist and he does not miss a chance to hurt and discredit God and His children. This book will show how to remove those legal rights and entry points and close those doors through the spiritual legal process of recognizing, renouncing, confessing, blessing and casting out.

Spiritual warfare is not just a fragment of Christianity; it is the whole of the Christian experience. It encompasses everything we do. To be a Christian is to be a spiritual warrior. To be a spiritual warrior is to walk consistently and victoriously through life with the Lord Jesus Christ. We, the Body of Christ, need to be educated as to the truth about spiritual warfare and how to effectively handle the weapons of that warfare.

Part I
What the Bible Says About Deliverance from Demons

What is a Deliverance Ministry?

Much of Jesus' Ministry Was Deliverance

Although references to demons being cast out in the Gospels were hastily passed over and assumed to be of little relevance to Christians in the 20th Century Church, truth cannot be suppressed forever (Horrobin13). There needs to be a re-emergence of the deliverance ministry in the 21st Century if we are to be a bride without spot or wrinkle. With occult activity on the rise, the morals of society in decline and terrorism an everyday occurrence, Christians are beginning to realize once again that living in this world is defiling and that deliverance needs to be a normal part of life.

Wherever Jesus went, miracles of deliverance happened. Jesus proclaimed that these same signs would follow all believers.

"And these signs shall follow them that believe; in my name shall they cast out devils…" (Mark 16:17a).

But sadly, many believers are following the signs instead. In Luke 10:1-17 we read how Jesus sent out seventy believers to minister the Gospel and in verse 19 He told them:

"Behold, I give you authority to trample on serpents and scorpions, and over all the power of the enemy, and nothing shall by any means hurt you."

They came back rejoicing because they had been able to minister deliverance from demon forces to those in bondage. Jesus quickly straightened out their priorities, however, by reminding them that the primary thing was salvation (Luke 10:20).

How Jesus Dealt with Demons

People came to Jesus seeking healing for their sicknesses, but many times to accomplish this Jesus cast demons out of them. Apparently the people did not realize that some of their sicknesses and diseases had demonic roots. One remarkable characteristic of Jesus' ministry, from beginning to end, is that He never made a hard and fast distinction between healing peoples' sicknesses and delivering them from demons. The same applies to His ongoing ministry of preaching, as described in Mark 1:39: *"And He preached in their synagogues throughout all Galilee, and cast out devils."* Casting out devils was as normal a part of Jesus' ministry as preaching and was both the confirmation and practical application of His message. His ministry proved over and over the reality of evil spirits. He came to destroy the works of the devil (1 John 3:8).

God's Word Is Our Authority

"All Scripture is given by inspiration of God, and is profitable for doctrine, for reproof, for correction, for instruction in righteousness: that the man of God may be complete, thoroughly equipped for every good work" (2 Timothy 3:16-17).

It is clear from reading this portion of Scripture that it is the entire Bible (all Scripture) that provides the broad base upon which to build. Many believers, however, ignore instruction in regard to the enemy of our soul choosing to remain ignorant of Satan's devices (2 Corinthians 2:11). Those in need of deliverance seek help from deliverance counselors which is why we need to be prepared to help them by becoming knowledgeable and capable to see them through to freedom from sickness and oppression.

Spiritual authority is the understanding of who we, as Christians, in Christ Jesus and it is the understanding of our correct relationship to God the Father as well (Garrison 29).

What Does "Deliverance" Mean?

In the Bible we see several uses of the word deliverance: Deliverance from sin and sickness, deliverance from self or the flesh and the works thereof, and deliverance from demon bondage and other snares of the devil such as generational and other curses.

What Does the Word "Spirit" Mean?

In Scripture we see several uses of the word spirit: The Holy Spirit, the Comforter, the Spirit of God, angels and or the host of heaven.

- The human spirit, which is the "real person," the part of us that is "born again" when we get saved. Only those who are born-again believers can be deliverance counselors.

"Jesus answered and said unto him, verily, verily I say unto thee; Except a man be born again he cannot see the Kingdom of God" (John 3:3).

- Spirit as in attitude or state of existence.

- Evil spirits, unclean, infirm, seducing demons, fallen angels, and the devil's angels. They are all extremely organized to invade mankind (Ephesians 6:11,12, Matthew 12:43-45).

In this book, the words demon, devil, evil spirit and unclean spirit are used to describe the satanic entities that harass and torment human beings. The terms are used interchangeably. Also, when reference is made to "casting out" it does not necessarily imply that all demonic spirits inhabit or "possess" humans. Although this is true in some cases the more common instance is that the person is being mentally or physically tormented or oppressed in some way. This type of torment is often in the mind of the individual and is brought to bear from the outside.

Psychology and Deliverance

Many Christians, who are suffering some kind of oppression, do not realize that the Bible provides for deliverance and they will often go to secular psychologists, psychiatrists or counselors believing that these people, with no biblical training can help them. There is a measure of help from them because they teach us to live with the demons and medicate them. Sometimes medication is necessary to bring the person to a point where he or she is lucid enough to receive ministry. However, Jesus died on the cross so we could become completely free; *"Free indeed"* (John 8:31, 32). God's way is to close the door and cast the demons out. Yes, we can cast out "disorders" and "phobias" (2 Corinthians 7:1) and many other diagnoses in the DSM IV. The DSM IV is the Diagnostic and Statistical Manual of Mental Disorders, forth revision of the handbook. Psychiatrists, psychologists and mental health professionals use this manual that lists different categories of mental disorders and the criteria for diagnosing them, to give a label to a disorder for the purposes of third party insurance billing.

If a mental health professional is needed, it is wise to find a Christian counseling specialist who has spent many hours preparing to transcend the confusion faced by clients. One who has learned to integrate Christian theology and psychological techniques to help the Christian grow spiritually as well as emotionally. These Christian counselors' beliefs saturate their counseling methods and they respect and honor people's Christian values while helping them understand and heal their emotional pain.

What is Truth?

God's Word is Truth

In today's educational system we are taught to have faith in man's wisdom and man's word instead of the Word of God. In our schools and universities today students are being taught WHAT to think, rather than how to think. Because of this, many are not sure that the Bible is the Word of God. They say there are too many things in the Bible that are not reasonable, or naturally possible.

When Pilate asked, "WHAT IS TRUTH?" (John 18:37, 38). He was most probably confused by all the religions and philosophies of the day clamoring for recognition. He did not stay to get an answer and in this he is like millions today who do not honestly seek to know truth, but follow every wind of doctrine that comes along. Christ is the Truth and anyone who finds Him and obeys Him will know the truth (John 8:32).

It is so important for us to stay in the Scriptures because we must see them with our eyes (a gate into our spirit), say them with our mouth and hear them with our ears (other spirit gates). It is then that we are able to use God's Word as a weapon against the enemy.

In John 8:31, 32 Jesus said we must "abide" in His Word if we want to get free.Free from the second death, from sin, from sickness, from demonic oppression, from poverty, curses and bondage. Abiding is dwelling, remaining. We must dwell and remain in God's Word.

What is truth? While talking to God the Father, Jesus said, "...*thy word is Truth*" (John 17:13-17). When Thomas asked Jesus to answer life's great question, "...*how can we know the way?*" Jesus saith unto him, "*I am the way, the truth and the life*" (John 14:5, 6). It is important to understand that many conditions that we may experience are facts, but may not the *truth*.

God's Word Has in It Creative Power

"*In the beginning was the Word and the Word was with God, and the Word was God. The same was in the beginning with God. All things were made by Him, and without Him nothing was made that was made*" (John 1:1-3).

In the Book of Genesis, Chapter 1, God spoke the entire universe into existence. God's Word has the ability to create. God created everything from nothing with words — even what we call the laws of physics and spiritual laws as well. He created them and He is well able to manipulate them through us! How does God release faith through us? By way of HIS words repeated from our mouth! God's Word will never change,

"*Forever, O Lord, thy Word is settled in heaven*" (Psalms 119:89),

but our circumstances can change. If we keep repeating

something over and over, we can create circumstances, positive or negative, with our words or with God's Word.

The Power of God's Word Delegated to Believers

God's power has been delegated to us in the Name of Jesus (John 14:12-14). He created the universe with words and all the elements of the universe, wood, metal, flesh... they all must respond to God's Word when it is spoken in faith, believing (Exodus 7:10; 2 Kings 6:6; Acts 3:6).

God created Satan and his demons as well, so they must also respond to God's Word (Mark 16:17; James 4:7). It is with the Word of God, spoken through us that we are able to bring about healing and deliverance in our life or in the life of another. We are justified or condemned by our words. Life and death are in the power of the tongue. We can bring blessing or cursing with our words.

Be a Doer of God's Word

James said that we should be doers of God's Word (James 1:22). It is the mouth of the upright that shall deliver them (Proverbs 12:6). It is not enough to give mental assent to God's Word. We must never say, I know God can, but rather, speak with authority saying, I know God will! It IS God's will to deliver from demons and snares of the devil. We must never pray if it is Thy will when praying for healing and deliverance. When we pray "IF" it shows doubt and doubt cancels faith. Jesus said we could cast out devils if we are believers (Mark 16:17). God never told anyone to do something that was impossible.

The Deliverance Ministry of Jesus

Jesus Went About Healing and Casting Out Devils

Mark begins his record of the ministry of Jesus with an incident in which a demon challenged Him as He was teaching in a synagogue in Galilee. The encounter spread His fame throughout the entire area (Mark 1:21-28). From that point on, we see Jesus dealing with demons wherever He encountered them during the three and a half years of His public ministry.

Jesus then commissioned His followers and delegated His authority to them. He never sent anyone out to preach the gospel without specifically instructing and equipping them to take action against devils in the same way that He did. There is no basis in the New Testament for an evangelistic ministry that does not include the expelling of demons. This is as true today as it was in the time of Jesus. The primary message of the gospel is salvation, however, in the Bible there are other messages and ministries as well. This includes the ministries of healing and deliverance. Jesus stood over Peter's mother-in-law,

"And He stood over her, and rebuked the fever; and immediately she arose and ministered unto them" (Luke 4:39).

He did not heal her from some natural problem, causing the fever, but He rebuked a spirit. It was a demon spirit that was causing her fever. Again in Luke 13:16 we read:

"And ought not this woman, being a daughter of Abraham, whom Satan hath bound, lo these eighteen years, be loosed from this bond?"

Then in Mark 5 we find recorded:

"There met him out of the tombs a man with an unclean spirit...For he said unto him, Come out of the man, thou unclean spirit," and in Mark 1 we read: "They brought unto him all that were diseased, and them that were possessed with devils...And he healed many that were sick of divers diseases, and cast out many devils..."

Jesus is our teacher and example and much of His ministry on earth was healing people's diseases and delivering them from demon bondage. In Luke 4:18 Jesus said He was fulfilling prophecy, being sent to preach deliverance to the captives. He had just finished His encounter with Satan in the wilderness where He shows us in Luke 4:1-13 that the weapon to use against Satan, his oppression and evil suggestions is simply God's Word. Then He said in Luke 4:18:

"The spirit of the Lord is upon me because he hath anointed me to preach the gospel to the poor; he hath sent me to heal the broken hearted, to preach deliverance to the captives and recovering of sight to the blind, to set at liberty them that are bruised."

The people of Jesus' day, much like our third world countries today, did not question the existence of evil spirits. In Matthew 15:22 a woman of Canaan came to Jesus bringing her daughter whom she said was *"grievously vexed with a devil."* Notice that she did not say her daughter was a paranoid schizophrenic, bi-polar or borderline. She did not say that her daughter was ADHD, an addict, an alcoholic, or that she had anxiety attacks. She simply stated that her daughter was *"damion izoma;"* miserably possessed and controlled by a demon. The woman, even without having extensive knowledge of these things called it what it was, a demon. While all these disorders can be the result of an imbalance in brain chemistry or hormones, they also have demonic roots. Demons can change brain chemistry. Cast the demon out and the brain chemistry can come into balance.

In Mark 5:2-20, Jesus ministered to the man of Gadara. The evil spirits controlling the man argued, but Jesus cast them out anyway. In verse 17 we read that this miracle troubled the people and they asked Him to leave. In Mark 1:23-27 Jesus ministered deliverance to a member of the synagogue right in front of the congregation. Jesus was teaching by demonstration, but the people said, *"What new doctrine is this?"* People still ask the same question today when they are unfamiliar with the Scriptures. Deliverance is not a new doctrine! Read Isaiah 61:1. What method did Jesus use? SIMPLY WORDS! God also created angels who rebelled and became evil; therefore, because they are part of God's creation, they also have no choice but to respond to God's Word.

How Jesus Taught Deliverance

Jesus taught by "words of instruction" in Matthew

12:22-30; 43-45. These Scriptures are explanations and cautions for the deliverance counselor. Jesus said that we cast out demons by the Spirit of God, not by Beelzebub (the devil).

He taught by "demonstration." In Luke 13:11-16 Jesus explained that the affliction of this particular believer was the work of an infirm spirit. He did not call it a congenital defect, but rather, He called it a spirit of infirmity. Jesus backed up His word with a demonstration. He cast it out and the woman stood up straight.

Jesus taught by the "now you go and do it method." In Luke 10:1 He sent out seventy and He sent them out two by two to be doers of the Word. In Verse 17 they returned rejoicing because they too had been able to minister deliverance. Jesus had to remind them, however, that the most important part of their ministry was salvation.

The Great Commission: Our Power of Attorney

First, Jesus ordained and delegated authority to the disciples sending them out two by two (Luke 9:1; 10:1), then, to all believers (Matthew 28:17-20; Mark 16:17; Luke 10:19). Then, He spoke words of caution and advice concerning that authority.

Jesus taught that it is possible for Satan to get an advantage over us if we are ignorant of his devices (2 Corinthians 2:11). The Bible tells us in 1 Peter 5:8 that we are to: *"Be sober, be vigilant; because your adversary the devil, as a roaring lion, walketh about, seeking whom he may devour."* We must cleanse ourselves from all filthiness of the flesh and the spirit (2 Corinthians 7:1). We must give NO place to the devil (Ephesians 4:17-32). We must submit to God *and also* resist the devil. Then he will flee from us (James 4:7).

We must stop fighting in the flesh and start fighting in the spirit. We must keep on our spiritual armor and start using our spiritual weapons (Ephesians 6:11-18). Once we get ourselves delivered and free of bondages, snares, curses, unclean spirits, fleshly habits, and all the other ways of the world, it will be much easier to minister deliverance to others. Jesus will assist the truly honest believer to get into the right position in Him (John 1:12, Philippians 4:13).

Demons and the Human Experience

What Are Demons and Where Do They Come From?

In preparing to go into combat a soldier studies everything about the enemy. We must do the same with our spiritual enemy. So, what can we learn from the Bible as to whom and what these entities are?

Demons are disembodied spirit beings that have an intense craving to occupy physical bodies (Prince 89). The word demon means evil spirit or devil. The word devil is used of Satan, the prince of devils (Matthew 9:34; 12:24). He is the chief devil and the original source of evil in the universe. There is only one prince but many demons. Satan has an angelic body and cannot enter bodily into anyone; but demons, as disembodied spirits do not seem to be able to operate in the material world except by inhabiting and through possession of bodies of men or beasts. They can also implement and carry out their diabolical deeds by influencing the mind.

There are two classes of fallen angels: Those who are bound in the bottomless pit (Revelation 9:11-14; 11:7; 17:8; 2 Peter 2:4; Jude 6-7) and those who are still loose with Satan and who will be cast down to the earth in the middle of Daniels's 70th week in the future tribulation (Revelation 12:7-12; Ephesians 6:10-17). The reason some of Satan's angels are now bound can be found in (2 Peter 2:4; Jude 6-7); Genesis 6:1-4).

God created angels to minister to Him and to us. These are spirit beings, personalities without physical bodies but with invisible, spirit ones (Hebrews 1:6-14). Lucifer was the most beautiful angel who rebelled and tried to overthrow God's throne. War in heaven was the result of this rebellion and he was cast out. He became the prince of devils (Isaiah 14:12-15). One third of all the angels followed Lucifer and they suffered the same fate. They became evil spirits (Revelation 12:4-9; Jude 6). Jesus was actually an eyewitness to this event before His incarnation (Luke 10:18). We should not pay Satan any respect in the sense of offering homage, for believers have been delivered from the domain of darkness, and transferred to the kingdom of His beloved Son (Colossians 1:13). We place ourselves in grave danger, however, if we are not aware of the wiles of the enemy (Horrobin 56).

How Did Rebellion Affect These Spirit Creatures?

These creatures had to give up their abode in heaven and apparently, they had to give up their bodies as well which would explain why they now seek new bodies in which to express themselves in every evil way that is diametrically opposed to God. They are intelligent, but evil, unclean, and extremely deceptive and seducing. Their activities are continually increasing exponentially as time for the return of Christ approaches (1Timothy 4:1, 2; 2 Peter 3:3, 4: Matthew 12:43-45). God has created men and angels to be free moral agents, an angel of God would never try to get into us or control us.

The Nature of Demons

Demons are just like their leader Satan in most ways. They are also very much like people in many ways as well. The Living Translation of the Bible refers to them as "people without bodies."

"For we are not fighting against people made of flesh and blood, but against persons without bodies – the evil rulers of the unseen world, those mighty satanic beings and great evil princes of darkness who rule this world; and against huge numbers of wicked spirits in the spirit world (Ephesians 6:12).

It is possible to tell how demonized a person is by noting how much of the following demonic characteristics are evident in his or her life.

- Demons are evil (Judges 9:23; 1 Samuel 18:10); intelligent and wise, but liars (1 Kings 22:21-24; know some of the future (Acts 16:16); powerful (Mark 5:1-18); disembodied spirits (Revelation 16:13-16); and they are individuals (Mark 16:9).

- They possess knowledge (Matthew 8:29; Luke 4:41) and they can identify and recognize people and family members (familiar spirits). Jesus and Paul are examples (Acts 19:15). This is how fortunetellers operate.

- They have feelings (Matthew 8:29), strong emotions (Acts 8:7; Mark 9:26), desires and preferences (Matthew 8:31; Luke 8:31), a will and the power of choice (2 Timothy 2:26; Matthew 12:43-45).

- They believe (James 2:19), and desire a friendly, but evil, fellowship and relationship with people (1 Corinthians 10:20; Leviticus 20:6).

- They have lustful desires and are alluring. They entice, seduce and tempt (2 Timothy 3:13), and have strong false beliefs or doctrines that they seek to impose upon us (1 Timothy 4:1, 2; 1 John 4:6). They are quite religious and go to Church regularly (Mark 1:23; 2 Corinthians 11:13-15; Revelation 2:9 and 3:9).

- They get raging angry, violent and vexed when rejected or refused (Mark 9:20-26; Matthew 15:22; 17:15; Luke 6:18; Acts 5:16). They are insanely jealous (Numbers 5:14 and 30; 1 Samuel 18:7- 11).

- Demons will take revenge, they strike back, retaliate, persecute and punish (1 Peter 5:8; Acts 10:38; Revelation 2:10). They influence people to betray and become traitors (John 13:2). They tell lies and influence people to do the same (Acts 5:3; 1 Kings 22:23).

- They try to make their opponents fearful (2 Timothy 1:7). That is the reason why they make those they oppress or possess, look so dreadful when in an angry rage.

- They are thieves. They steal and teach those they oppress the tricks of the trade (Luke 8:12; John 10:10).

- Like Humans, demons have a certain degree of the fear of God (James 2:19). They are worldly and fashion minded (1 Corinthians 2:12; 1 John 2:15-17) and very proud (Ezekiel 28:17).

- They have degrees of wickedness (Matthew 12:45; Luke 8:2; 11:26) and have varying degrees of un-cleanness and filthiness (Luke 6:18). They have supernatural powers to do miracles and perform outstanding feats (Revelation 16:14). They can teach and instruct others (1Timothy 4:1) and they can bring discord, division, lying, and strife between people (Matthew 13:38, 39; 1 Kings 22:21-24).

Christians Are Not Impervious to Demon Bondage

NO! We are not impervious to Satan. That is what he wants us to think so as to keep us from dealing effectively with our problems. Some are under the impression that a

Christian needs only to deal with the flesh. While it is true that we cannot cast out the flesh, neither can we crucify a demon! The believer must determine the cause before he or she can apply the cure. There is a difference between Christ's provision and our appropriation of that provision.

Provision and Appropriation

Christ defeated Satan and triumphed over him and his demons, yet Christians are still vexed and tormented. Deliverance must also be appropriated (Joel 2:32). Christ bore the sins of all, yet all are not saved. Salvation must be received and then appropriated. Christ took our infirmities and bore our sicknesses, but many Christians are still sick. Healing must be received and then appropriated. Christ sent the comforter, the Holy Spirit, to baptize us with power and yet all believers have not received the baptism of the Holy Spirit. It also must be received and appropriated.

The Armor of God

The routine of putting on the full armor significantly reduces the likelihood of fatal injury and greatly increases battlefield effectiveness (Weber 162). If an individual has been taken captive, he or she must acknowledge the truth of God's Word to get free (2 Timothy 2:25, 26). We need the whole spiritual armor of God in order to withstand the spiritual weapons of Satan, but it is left up to the individual whether it is worn at all times (Ephesians 6:11-18). The devil hates us because he does not own us and because he hates our Father, God.

Some will give heed to seducing spirits (1 Timothy 4:1). Some will have their minds corrupted and actually receive an unclean spirit (2 Corinthians 11:3, 4). Satan can get advantage of us if we choose to remain ignorant of his methods (2 Corinthians 2:11). He will try to deceive us by having his men appear righteous and minister to us (2 Corinthians 11:13-15). Darts of doubt and deception must be immediately met by faith. The shield extinguishes every flaming arrow of the enemy when we actively apply truth to our situation (Ingram 129). Using our armor and getting right before God is important if we want to be able to counsel others. Once set free it will be possible to use the truths of Scripture to help others who may also have been taken captive.

Who Has Power and Authority Over Demons?

Every "*born again*" believer has power and authority over the enemy (John 1:12). There is no reason for a child of God to be fearful or to hesitate to take authority over devils when a person is being tormented. Don't be intimidated, just do it! The provision has been made (Luke 10:19), but it must be appropriated (James 4:7).

What is the Destiny of Demon Spirits?

Satan and his evil demon spirits are ultimately doomed to spend eternity in hell (Isaiah 14:12-15: Matthew 25:41). In the meantime, the believer must *occupy* this world with boldness and authority for his or her own liberty as well as for that of brothers and sisters in Christ (Ephesians 6:18).

Discerning Spirits

What Does Discerning of Spirits Mean?

Discerning is the power of perception, insight, or the power of seeing clearly. Hence, discerning of spirits is the ability to distinguish between the work of the Holy Spirit, an unclean evil spirit, and the human spirit.

Discerning of spirits is not a natural ability but is one of the supernatural gifts of the Holy Spirit listed in the 12th Chapter of 1 Corinthians. This gift provides the "eyes of the Church." It is needed to cope with the powers of hell that are out to destroy the Church and the individual.

Spiritual Gifts as Credentials

Spiritual gifts are the credentials of the believer. Natural man is a prisoner of his senses, but spiritual man, the born-again, Holy Spirit-baptized believer, has access to spiritual power needed to live in supernatural victory and to cope with a supernatural enemy. Jesus said in Mark 16 that it is only normal for the signs to follow a believer who is willing to appropriate the promises.

Jesus taught by demonstration. We often hear sermons about what Jesus and the disciples did, but little about how they did it and how it relates to us personally today. Jesus, through the Holy Spirit, empowers other believers with the same signs and credentials (Acts 8:5-7). Some will say, "Don't ask for proof, only believe." Jesus pointed out that the signs, which were the credentials, should be evidence (Matthew 10:8; Mark 16:17-20; John 10:25).

The Gifts of the Holy Spirit

Each gift of the Holy Spirit is a God given ability placed within us when we are baptized in the Holy Spirit and are manifestations of the Holy Spirit. They are for our benefit and profit. We are expected to exercise them. They will not be taken away from us (1 Corinthians 12:4-7; Acts 3:6; Romans 11:29).

In the 12th Chapter of 1 Corinthians we are told much about the importance of the gifts. We are told that they are good gifts, that they are from God and that we are not to be ignorant of them. The gifts glorify God and establish the faith of the believer. The gifts impart faith, blessings, healing and deliverance.

How do we get the gifts to manifest? God knows which gifts are important to each one's specific ministry (1 Corinthians 12:11). They must be desired (1 Corinthians 12:31). They may come naturally (1 Corinthians 12:11). They may come by the laying on of hands (2 Timothy 1:6).

We must not, however, confuse the function of ministries with gifts. Those functions mentioned for the parts of the Body of Christ in 1 Corinthians 12:27-30 are various ministries for which the gifts are required. They are not the gifts themselves.

The Nine Gifts of the Holy Spirit

Grouped into three categories they are:

The revelation gifts:
1) Word of wisdom, 2) word of knowledge, 3) discerning of spirits.

The utterance gifts:
1) Tongues, 2) interpretation, 3) prophecy.

The power gifts:
1) Faith, 2) healings, 3) working of miracles.

The presence of an unclean spirit is detected by the gift of discerning of spirits. We cast them out with our words (utterances), by the gift of working of miracles. Yes, casting out an evil spirit is a miracle!

Operating in the Gifts

Jesus said in John 14:30 that Satan would find nothing in Him. We must apply that same test to ourselves. There must be no hatred, no jealousy, no bitterness, no pride, no anxiety for the future, and no deception. These will hinder ministry. If we are not open with the Lord, our mind can be shaken, deceived by satanic powers and given over to satanic delusion to where we could believe a lie (2 Thessalonians 2:2, 9 and 11).

Hatred toward self is another area that will need to be dealt with. We know that God is pleased when we have a humble and contrite heart. The pride of life and egotism erodes character. It is good to esteem others more highly than our self, but Satan will try to get one to demean self. He is the false accuser and he tries to accentuate the negative in a person's life and get him or her to hate self. When self-debasing starts to come in, one should cast it down and instead thank and praise God for every good thing in one's character and personality. God made just one of each person and He made each one for His own pleasure, then He broke the mold. We are wonderfully unique to Him and He loves each one with the same intensity and divine passion that He does the most brilliant person in the world (Otis 76).

We must be transparent before God. With an act of our will, we must determine with all our heart to obey God's Word and to be a co-worker with Him. With the gifts being simply manifestations of the Holy Spirit who is already within us, we simply need to "stir them up" (2 Timothy 1:6).

To understand discerning of spirits remember that God is a spirit (John 4:24), angels are spirits (Hebrews 1:7), Satan is a spirit (Ephesians 2:2), demons are spirits (Luke 10:17), and men and women are spirits (James 2:26). Every counselor needs to be able to operate in the gift of discerning of spirits. With this gift the counselor has the ability to know which spirit he or she is dealing with and whether the power at work is power from God or from Satan. God will identify names of demons, if we ask Him, so we can cast them out by name. If the problem is the flesh we will be able to counsel on how to crucify the flesh as well.

Detection of Evil Spirits by Evidence

There are four major groups of demons that attack humans: Principalities, powers, rulers of the darkness of this world and spiritual wickedness in high places (Ephesians 6:12). These must be bound when they attempt to block deliverance.

Infirm and unclean spirits attack the mind and the body.

Unclean spirits affect a person in three major ways: 1) by enslaving, 2) by defiling and, 3) by tormenting.

By some simple observations, with the assistance of the gift of discerning of spirits, the counselor can usually tell what spirits are present and operating in a person's life. Some behavior and states of mind are most assuredly of God and some are not. By making comparisons, it will be possible to identify what evil spirits need to be cast out. Following is an example of some of those comparisons. The list is for example only and is by no means exhaustive.

Evidence of Satan	Evidence of God
Unbelief in God's Word	Faith/belief in God's Word
Disobedience and rebellion	Obedience and compliance
Emotional disturbances	A sound, healthy mind
Unclean thoughts and dreams	Pure thoughts and dreams
Urge to destroy	Urge to edify and build
Fears and phobias	Peace, courage and serenity
Superiority and inferiority	Humility, Assurance and confidence

The Legal Transaction of Renouncing

Renouncing the Hidden Things of Dishonesty

To renounce means to give up formally, to cast off and disown, and to "take back." As it applies to deliverance, it is casting off, disowning and getting rid of some memory, some curse, some circumstance, or some hidden sin of dishonesty which produced the invitation for demon visitation whether it was in childhood or adulthood (2 Corinthians 4:2). Renouncing sets the stage for deliverance so that counselees may recover from the snares of the devil (2 Timothy 2:25, 26).

Attacking Satan with the spoken word is necessary, as it is the *mouth* of the upright person that delivers him (Proverbs 12:6). Some experience deliverance at salvation. Some experience more deliverance when they are baptized in the Holy Spirit. They *speak* their heavenly language and their problems seem to disappear. With others, however, even after the baptism, they still have the same problems with the mental torment and the fear. They remain addicted, tormented, oppressed and harassed.

These people may have laid their lives down for Christ and have really prayed to crucify the flesh, but their problems still persist. Usually, the reason for this is because a door to the evil supernatural has been opened somewhere in their life or in their family lineage. This has caused the presence of demon bondages and snares of the devil and those doors must be closed and dealt with according to the Scriptures for deliverance to take place.

Knowledge, the Key to Closing the Doors to the Devil

God spoke in Isaiah 5:13 and said, "My people have gone into captivity because they have no knowledge." Again in Hosea 4:6 He said, "My people are destroyed for lack of knowledge." Ignorance is the only way in Scripture that the devil can bind up and destroy a child of God. The ignorance of the victim is the devil's only real power. This book will provide the knowledge that is necessary to set Christians free from bondage.

Some have received ministry for deliverance and must come back for more deliverance time and time again. Proverbs 26:2 teaches us that "The curse causeless shall not come" so there has to be an open door for the enemy to have a legal right to keep coming back. These people need extreme patience on the part of the deliverance counselor. It is with the gift of discerning of spirits that we are able to ascertain whether it is simply fear or lack of knowledge that is holding them in bondage or if that person is still in sin. If sin is still in his or her life, the sin must be dealt with if they are to receive any more deliverance.

If a counselee is not in sin, but still experiencing spirit visitations, remind him or her that Exodus 23:28-30 tells us that it is little by little that the enemy is driven out, as we are able to possess the land within us so they are to be patient. Total deliverance does not always come all at once, but we hold the key. The more determined we are to fill ourselves with God's Word and obey it, thus possessing our land; the sooner we can be free of the enemy.

The Legal Process

There are five very important steps in the deliverance process. 1) Recognize, 2) renounce, 3) confess, 4) bless, 5) cast out.

Recognize: If the problem is demonic recognize how ground was given and doors opened. Ask the Holy Spirit, He will help in this process.

Renounce: The problem is a lie of the devil. Renounce the lie and the situation that gave ground and opened doors. Renounce them one by one (Ephesians 4:27; 2 Corinthians 4:1, 2; 2 Timothy 2:25).

Confess: Counselees must confess the promise in God's Word that states his or her situation, as it *should* be. Decree it and it shall be established (Job 22:28). Then replace the lie with the truth (2 Corinthians 4:2; 2 Timothy 2:25).

Bless: Those who may have proclaimed curses on the counselee must be blessed one by one. Then, it is important to forgive them (Luke 6:28). Forgive them even if they are no longer living. The story in Judges 17:1, 2 is a perfect example of why we are to bless those that curse us.

"And there was a man of mount Ephraim, whose name was Micah. And he said unto his mother, the eleven hundred shekels of silver that were taken from thee, about which thou cursedst, and spakest of also in mine ears, behold,

the silver is with me; I took it. And his mother said, Blessed be thou of the Lord, my son."

That man's mother knew how to break a curse. She knew that it would be broken by blessing her son whom she had previously cursed.

Cast Out: After laying the foundation, the spirits are cast out, one by one. It is very important that prayer should be by Holy Spirit filled believers (Mark 16:17, 18). Also read Acts 19:13-17 and be cautioned.

Organize an index of alphabetized cards with Scriptures relating to the common bondages that will likely be encountered. Use these Scriptures to combat and counterattack Satan and his demons by having the counselee read them in his or her Bible. No list can be totally complete; as certain Scriptures will be quickened and the Holy Spirit will reveal the ones needed while ministering to the individual. Use the following list as an example. The index will build with research.

Rejection	Ephesians 1:6
Rebellion	Ephesians 6:1-3
Poverty	3 John 1:2
Infirmities	Matthew 8:17
Heredity curses	Galatians 3:13
Fear and insanity	2 Timothy 1:7
Guilt and shame	Romans 8:1

Unforgiveness	Matthew 6:12
Lying	Proverbs 12:19
Homosexuality	Romans 1:24-28
Lust	1 Corinthians 9:27; 2 Timothy 2:22
Unclean thoughts	Philippians 4:8
Witchcraft and occult	Deuteronomy 18:10-12
Drugs	Romans 12:1; Revelation 18:23

Scriptural Reasons to Use This Five-Step Procedure

There are Scriptural benefits from following this process. Satan's access to the person's life is removed (Ephesians 4:27). The deliverance is much more likely to be permanent, providing the individual will obey God's New Covenant and not re-open the door by re-committing sin. Remember that Jesus said,

"IF you continue in My Word, THEN you shall know the truth and the truth shall make you free" (John 8:31, 32).

The promise of deliverance, like most of the other promises in God's Word, is conditional.

With this procedure curses are broken (Luke 6:28), casting out the spirits will be easier, and there will be fewer manifestations experienced. Remember that the Christian counselor has the authority. Do not allow any demonic manifestations to take place. Satan's footing will be gone so demons have no alternative but to leave because their legal rights to be there have been removed (James 4:7).

NEVER converse with evil spirits. They will try to draw and tempt Christians into conversations but any information they give will probably be lies anyway because they are liars! It is much safer to consult the Holy Spirit and He will instruct and give all the needed information.

The Interview with Two or Three Witnesses

A contract or covenant, is binding when executed in the presence of witnesses. It is therefore desirable that while ministering deliverance two or three people be present. Deuteronomy 19:15; 2 Corinthians 13:1 and Matthew 18:16 all say in effect that in the presence of two or three witnesses a matter is established legally. This is a legal principle and it is a Scriptural principle.

The enemy would like to deceive us into believing that remembering and renouncing incidents is digging up old sins that God has forgiven. On the contrary, this process is not digging up old sins, but drilling down to the infection of those old sins. We must not give heed to this seducing spirit. If the incident was in fact a sin, God has forgiven and forgotten. Satan, on the other hand, has not. We are simply closing the door officially. The curse causeless does not come. There is a reason for the tormented person's problems.

Every psychologist, psychiatrist, or mental health counselor begins the counseling session by asking questions and helping the patient to "deal with" their past. Jesus wants us to deal with our past His way, by the five step procedure previously discussed.

Every time we see a physician for the first time he begins by asking about our habits, whether or not we smoke, take drugs, or drink. He takes us through a long list of physical conditions that we, personally, or someone in our family might have had. Even medical doctors know about curses, they just don't know that they know. Without spiritual eyes open they can only see the physical. If they are not Christians they do not have the gift of discerning of spirits so they can't connect the dots. Every health care professional knows that an infection must heal from the inside out.

Schizophrenia, the Double Mind

The Split Personality

The goal of this section is to focus on the spiritual aspects of this mental disorder and to look at schizophrenia from a spiritual perspective to see some spiritual solutions.

Schizophrenia is a disintegration of the development of the personality. A mental disorder characterized by withdrawal and aggression, elation and depression, a dual personality. The Bible calls it double mindedness (James 1:8; 4:7, 8).

In looking at schizophrenia from a spiritual perspective we can see that many characteristics of this "mental disorder" actually relate more to the spiritual area. Therefore, spiritual solutions must exist.

Fear is not of God (2 Timothy 1:7), yet many who suffer from schizophrenia experience extreme fear. Their visions are often gruesome and tormenting. Often the person uses extreme profanity. However, the Word says that we are to avoid profane words (1 Timothy 6:20). The individual also may hear voices that may suggest and promote (1) shameful behavior, (2) self-condemnation, and (3) violent, destructive behavior. In contrast, the Word says that we are to test the spirits (1 John 4:1) and to avoid such behavior (Ephesians 4:22-23). One may feel as if he or she has committed the unpardonable sin and that God is out to get them. In contrast, the Word says that through Jesus we can have forgiveness and cleansing of all our sins (1 John 1:9 and Isaiah 1:18).

The Double Mind

Schizophrenia victims often exhibit a divided mind or double mind. In fact, the original meaning of the term "schizophrenia" carries the idea of a "divided personality". The Word of God speaks to the issue of being double minded (James 1:8). Confusion is another major characteristic of schizophrenia, but God is not the author of confusion (1 Corinthians 14:33). Since those who have this disorder are poor in logic, there must be a breakdown of constructs in their minds.

The Possible Causes of Schizophrenia

The onset of this malady is common during the late teens. These are the critical years of life. Traumatic experiences, rejection and rebellion are often door openers along with failures in school, work, and social relationships. Those suffering from this ailment usually live in a fantasy world, detached from reality. However, Scripture says that we are to cast down vain imaginations and to bring every thought captive (2 Corinthians 10:5).

The Dynamics of Rejection and Rebellion

The deepest bruise that can be inflicted by our enemy is the bruise of rejection (Thompson 19). This demon is a control spirit and must be bound. He has two main subordinates, rejection and rebellion and they both must be bound and cast out. The primary job of these devil captains is to set up opposing personalities within an individual. Amos 3:3 says, "*Can two walk together lest they be agreed?*" They can't, and this is the cause of the mental turmoil within the schizophrenic. Rejection is often the beginning. Rejection can enter as early as in the womb if the child was not wanted, or was not the gender desired by the parents. Perhaps the child was a disappointment in other ways. Rejection causes anger and the door is open to rebellion. These demons are the doormen who allow all the others to enter and by the teen years, schizophrenia begins to manifest. Rebellion then goes to work in setting up his side of the personality, inviting spirits that oppose the nature of those accompanying rejection. Anger is manifested against those the person should love. The resultant life manifestations are such that the schizophrenic life is a series of storms, inner and outer turmoil. The personality observed is usually not the person at all, but one or more of the spirits. The person often wonders who he or she really is. The real personality has never been allowed to develop. It is submerged in a sea of demonic activity. There are really three personalities present, rejection, rebellion and the true person which is submerged.

The Battle Plan for Deliverance

The person in the bondage of schizophrenia faces a somewhat different and more difficult deliverance than the ordinary in that he or she cannot be set free all at once. Deliverance for the schizophrenic is like peeling an onion. The old personalities must come off one layer at a time. As the real personality is gradually revealed, little by little (Exodus 23:24-33) the person must come to grips with who he or she now is. As that occurs, another layer can be peeled off. Deliverance may take an extended period of time and may depend upon how involved the person is and how determined he or she is to grow in the Lord. In counseling the person who has been tormented by this demon it is wise to gently confront the lies, fantasies, and deception with the Word of God.

It will be necessary to break generational curses and help the person come to understand who she or she is in Christ. Minister healing for past hurts and direct the individual to learn how to build his or her real personality through Scripture memorization, meditation in the Word, the proper confession, and application. It is also important to teach the counselee how to establish proper communication and fellowship with God and also to help him or her to understand that it is possible and necessary to refuse to listen to voices. God will not speak to a person in this condition the same way He will speak to an unaffected person. He will speak mainly through Scripture. Also teach the importance of casting down vain imaginations and bringing every thought captive to the obedience of Christ. It is the renewing of the mind by replacing vain imaginations with the Word of God that will bring freedom. Long-term follow-up and accountability may be needed. The counselor must be open to the Holy Spirit so that he or she will be able to discern if and or when to refer the person to another professional. In some cases the use of drug therapy may be necessary to bring temporary relief. However, there is a danger of drugs masking the causes of the problems. Long-term use of medications also may hinder the potential healing and deliverance.

The Word of God is Sufficient

We should remember that the Word of God is sufficient to use in all types of counseling.

All Scripture is given by inspiration of God, and is profitable for doctrine, for reproof, for correction, for instruction in righteousness: That the man of God may be perfect, thoroughly furnished unto all good works (2 Timothy 3:16-17).

Living in Divine Order

The Importance of Divinely Ordered Husbands and Wives

The majority of evil spirits that enter into a person, or torment them from without, have gained access by circumstances and or by the sins of others as well as by the sins of the individual. Once a person is delivered, however, or even in the process of getting free, such as with schizophrenia it is vitally important that we walk in the light of God's Word to avoid being overtaken by darkness again.

The Scriptures show us that our prayers can be hindered if we do not live in divine order. We cannot draw from God's power and we will be out from under God's protection and will be subject to attack by Satan and his tormenting spirits. It is important to realize that we can go into bondage or be in danger of destruction because of ignorance of God's Word concerning divine order (Hosea 4:6 and Isaiah 5:13).

There cannot be divine order in a family if a born-again Christian marries an unsaved person (2 Corinthians 6:14). If already married to an unbeliever, pray for that mate's salvation. The mate is sanctified by the saved one's covenant with God (1 Corinthians 7:14). There are many evil spirits assigned to destroy marriages, which is all too evident by the ever-increasing rate of divorce, even in the Church.

When the family is out of divine order it often causes anger and rage to come into the marriage leading to domestic violence. A couple should enter into marriage knowing one another well enough that they, with the assurance and determination in both their hearts, that divorce is not an option and that with the Lord, there is nothing that cannot be worked out (Matthew 17:20).

Husbands and wives should make decisions together. The husband should be the primary disciplinarian (Hebrews 12:7-9; Colossians 3:21; Proverbs 19:18). He is to love and protect his wife (Ephesians 5:25-29; 1 Peter 3:7), even from the children. Love is a decision, not just an emotion.

He must be available emotionally to his wife and learn what that means to her. He must also be faithful to her as well (Hebrews 13:4). He must not bully his wife to be available sexually but husband and wife should be mutually available to one another and most importantly, agreeable. Nothing can "defile the marriage bed" worse than disagreements over what is to be permitted. If the husband is not fulfilling his proper role, the family loses its protection and every family member is open to evil supernatural attack.

Divinely Ordered Children

According to Anderson and Russo, the intrusion of the powers of darkness is very prevalent with our children. They questioned 286 students in one Christian high school and these startling responses were tabulated.

Forty-five percent said they have experienced a "presence" (seen or heard) in their room that scared them.

Fifty-nine percent said they have harbored bad thoughts about God.

Forty-three percent said they find it mentally hard to pray and read their Bible.

Sixty-nine percent reported hearing "voices" in their head, like there was a subconscious voice talking to them.

Twenty-two percent said they frequently entertain thoughts of suicide.

Seventy-four percent think they are different than others ("It works for others but not for me") (Anderson/Russo 33).

When children are not disciplined with consistency and taught to willingly function in their proper positions in the family, they become unprotected and open to demonic activity. Many children usurp their parent's God given authority over them and begin to have demonic visitation such as was discovered to occur in the Anderson/Russo study. Parents must not allow their children to rebel against authority because when they do, their protection from demonic attack is compromised.

Children are to honor their parents or they risk an early death (Ephesians 6:1-3; Hebrews 12:7-11). They must be disciplined in love. When children are disciplined they learn to keep their bodies and spirits under control (Proverbs 25:28). Learning to obey their parents will help children to more easily obey the Lord when they are grown. This will protect them in the future.

Our children are precious gifts from God. Let us do everything we can to protect them against the seductive schemes of the devil by being the parents God wants us to be, surrounding them with a Christ-centered home, and lifting them to God in prayer (Anderson/Russo 230).

The Divinely Ordered Individual

We are a trinity, a triune being. We <u>are</u> a SPIRIT who has a SOUL and lives in a BODY. We are spirit beings having a human experience. Our soul must willingly take the number two position and our body, number three, thus allowing our born-again spirit to rule. God speaks to us through our spirit. When our soul or our body usurps, transcends or ignores our spirit, we are out of order and unprotected. The results of this are spiritual and emotional ups and downs, depression, confusion, frustration, and the lack of joy, warfare within and without, torment, enslavement and defilement. *"Behold, his soul which is lifted up is not upright in him"* (Habakkuk 2:4).

Our SPIRIT is the part of us that was born-again by the indwelling of the Holy Spirit when we got saved (1 Peter 1:22-23). Our SOUL is like a computer that feeds the instructions to our body to perform deeds. This computer (soul) can only do what it is told to do by an instruction program. The instructions can come from God, Satan, or self.

God wants to write our computer program through our born-again spirit. He desires to feed into us data that will give us knowledge

"The wisdom from above is first pure, then peaceable, gentle, and easy to be entreated, full of mercy and good fruits, without partiality, and without hypocrisy" (James 3:17).

Satan wants to write our computer program through our mind; to feed into us data that will destroy us but:

"This wisdom descendeth not from above, but is earthly, sensual, and devilish. For where envying and strife is, there is confusion and every evil work" (James 3:15, 16).

Then there is self who also wants to write our program through our fleshly desires.

"To be carnally minded is death but to be spiritually minded is life and peace so they that are in the flesh cannot please God" (Romans 8:6-8).

Our BODY is our earth suit. That wonderfully created piece of machinery that provides a home for our spirit and our soul while we are here on earth, and performs deeds in response to directions it receives through our soul.

"I will praise thee; for I am fearfully and wonderfully made: Marvelous are they works; and that my soul knoweth right well" (Psalms 139:14).

The Divinely Ordered Soul

Our SOUL is a trinity also, made up of WILL, REASON and EMOTION. The will must be in control, *willing* to obey the Spirit of God. Reason is second in command and then the emotions. This is divine order with the soul.

Our WILL must be to obey the will of God. Jesus, our teacher and example spoke to God the Father and said, *"Nevertheless, not what I will, but what thou wilt"* (Mark 14:36). Our reasoning cannot always lead to proper decisions (1 Corinthians 3:19; Proverbs 14:12). Nor can our emotions alone lead to proper decisions (Deuteronomy 28:66, 67).

When the emotions are allowed to dominate the will, the soul is confused, unhappy, rebellious, frustrated and frightened. It wants to fight and cry and take dominion over the spirit and body and be disobedient to God's Word. It is evidenced by psychoses of every sort. The soul accepts the instructions from the wrong source.

"An angry man stirreth up strife, and a furious man aboundeth in transgression" (Proverbs 29:22).

Recognize the Condition and Recover

As deliverance counselors we must teach those we counsel that when we pray the Holy Spirit will reveal our personal condition. He will teach us and bring things to our remembrance needing attention that we thought we had forgotten (John 14:26). We can command our soul into order (1 Chronicles 22:19). We can speak to our soul (Psalms 62:5; Psalms 103:2; Psalms 42:5). Our soul can hear (Jeremiah 4:19). Our soul can talk back (Lamentations 3:24).

As we pray, the prayer of command should be out loud and with authority: Father, it is my will to submit to Your Word. I command myself to come into divine, upright order before God. I command my body to obey my soul, my soul to obey my spirit and my spirit to obey the Holy Spirit of God.

As counselors we must be sure that we are clean before the Lord. It is necessary that the counselor pray and fast on a regular basis and be sure that all sin is confessed. Praying in combination with fasting is spiritual warfare at its best. He or she must keep short accounts, forgiving others easily and quickly. It is imperative that the deliverance counselor do these things so he or she will be in a position spiritually to help others recover themselves out of the snares of the devil!

Part II
How We Open the Door to the Devil

Sinning With Our Words

Words and Thoughts

In Psalms 19:14 we read that the words of our mouth must be acceptable in the sight of God. There are good reasons for this - words are spirit (John 6:63). Words have creative power in them and because of this they must be used with great care. Words are like arrows (Psalms 64:1-8).

"Death and life are in the power of the tongue" (Proverbs 18:21).

We choose whether we shoot arrows of death or arrows of life (Deuteronomy 30:19).

Words are Things

God spoke everything into existence (Genesis 1). God spoke man into existence and then He delegated this power to man. Man is the only creature with the ability to speak God's Word. Man can speak positive words of God and bring forth a good creation to glorify God, or he can speak the opposite – negative words of Satan and bring forth an evil counterfeit which will glorify the devil. Even a born-again Christian can bring about satanic counterfeits with his or her words.

With our mouth we can speak God's Word, penetrate the body of an individual and carve out a problem (Hebrews 4:12). God's Words are sharper than a laser beam. They can cut away a spirit! God wants us to correct our way of talking and bring our words into line with His words so that we will have a good, blessed life.

When we speak God's Word, we invite the presence of the Holy Spirit and God's ministering angels. But when we speak Satan's words (even in ignorance or jest) we invite the presence of Satan and his demon spirits. The potential end of this is our destruction or bondage (Hosea 4:6; Isaiah 5:13).

Curses

The area of speaking curses is a less common but still a strong opening to demons. To curse someone is to ask for evil to happen to them. Those requests (really prayers) are heard by Satan and his forces and he answers them when possible. This includes everything from occult and witchcraft curses to one individual wishing harm on another. Balaam was paid to curse Israel, but God would not allow it (Numbers 22 - 24). Curses can also be passed on from generation to generation. The Bible says that speaking evil of someone is the same as cursing them (Romans 12:14). Things like: "I hope he dies..." "Since he/she won't love me I wish they would ....." "He is no good, and will never amount to anything..." "I hope she gets some of her own medicine..." "I hope her children do the same to her when they grow up." It is even possible to curse self with the wrong words (Proverbs 6:2). Our words are powerful and important. They are not something to be taken lightly.

Profanity

Using profanity (curse words) also falls into this category. When someone "damns" someone to "hell" demons love to hear it, they use the power of the hate in the speaker and will latch onto any open door that gave authority or justification to do their evil! If a person feels someone has cursed them, remember that they are to bless them that curse you (Matthew 5:44) and break that curse in Jesus' name, claiming Galatians 3:10, 13 which says,

"Christ redeemed us from the curse of the law by becoming a curse for us, for it is written, cursed is everyone who hangs on a tree."

Ask God to turn the curse to a blessing (Deuteronomy 23:5). A curse is an "evil wish" or a negative prayer. Even in ignorance it can bring on physical, mental, or circumstantial problems (Proverbs 26:2). Although it should not be, the tongue is the cause of curses. Out of the same mouth can come blessing or cursing (James 3:10). The use of our tongue is serious in God's eyes. Our tongue can be the key to our being justified (saved) or condemned (lost) (Matthew 12:36, 37). Our tongue is like the rudder of a ship. It can steer us to safety or it can steer us to destruction (James 3:1-10).

Controlling our Tongue

When we determine to control our tongue we can control our life and bring blessings to those we talk about. Words will control our spirit, our soul and our body. We need to ask ourselves if our mouth is disciplined. Are we inviting blessings or cursing? Following are some examples of the ungodly use of words that, if used often enough, can open doors that invite spirits to take up residence in a person.

- Calling someone stupid repeatedly could invite a spirit of stupidity to attack that person.

- Repeatedly telling a child that he cannot do things because he hasn't the ability could invite a spirit of inferiority to attach itself to him.

- Calling a daughter a whore could invite a spirit of prostitution to come in.

- Calling a person queer or fag could invite spirits of homosexuality to torment that person.

- Continually saying we are going crazy or that something or someone is driving us crazy could invite spirits of insanity to come upon us.

- Calling someone a witch could invite witchcraft spirits to attack.

- Telling someone to drop dead or wishing they were dead could call a death spirit to come upon that person.

Nicknames can also bring curses. Some may seem harmless but some nicknames are not as harmless as one might think. They can sometimes be foolish and dangerous because they can actually be names of spirits such as "Bugaboo" or "Chi-Chi" or "Python." Call someone by a name like these and we invite an evil spirit to attach itself to them. A person could actually take on the nature of the spirit. We are to take on the nature of Christ and be called by His Name.

Controlling Our Health with Our Words

Which do we say? I'm coming down with a virus, or I'm coming down with a healing. We need to confess the truth of God's Word in Matthew 8:17b,

"...Himself took our infirmities, and bare our sicknesses."

"My son, attend to my words; incline thine ear unto my sayings. Let them not depart from thine eyes; keep them in the midst of thine heart. For they are life unto those that find them, and health to all their flesh" (Proverbs 4:20-22).

"There is that speaketh like the piercings of a sword; but the tongue of the wise is health" (Proverbs 12:18),

"A wholesome tongue is a tree of life; but perverseness therein is a breach in the spirit (Proverbs 15:4).

You see, our mouth can be the cause of our ailments – or our healing. It is important to remember this and to teach counselees this truth.

The only absolute truth is the Word of God. If we are to experience all the blessings of God's promises, we must discipline ourselves to speak only this absolute truth and not speak the condition or the fact that we are experiencing. Our condition will change to coincide with God's Word IF we continue to speak God's Word (John 8:31, 32). 1 Peter 2:24 states:

"Who His own self bare our sins in His own body on the tree, that we, being dead to sins, should live unto righteousness; by whose stripes ye WERE healed." These are the words that should be coming out of our mouths.

Words Bind and Words Deliver

If the Lord has revealed that words have contributed to a person's problems, do not despair. While it is true that we can be snared by wrong words (study Proverbs 6:2), we are also set free by the proper use of words (study Proverbs

12:6). These are basic Scriptural truths. We can change our words and obtain freedom!

The devil will try to make us give place to him by tempting us to speak negative words, or by getting us to think and do things which are contrary to God's nature. We must stay clear of his devices and keep on our spiritual armor (Ephesians 6:13-18). We must call upon the Lord to initiate and keep our deliverance (Joel 2:32). It is entirely up to the individual when it comes to keeping his or her deliverance.

Sinning With Our Mind

Meditations of the Heart

The Bible shows us that our thoughts are just as critical as our words (Psalms 19:14). We are warned to discipline our minds to think on pure things (Philippians 4:8, 9). If we do not, we can give place to the devil. We must cast down imaginations. What we hear, read, think, or look at can put our imagination to work. We are warned to get this area under control and centered on holy things (2 Corinthians 10:3-5).

For our own protection we should look, listen, read and think on pure things (Philippians 4:8, 9). We must examine ourselves. What do we allow our mouth to say? What do we allow our eyes to see? What do we allow our ears to hear? What do we allow our mind to think? What do we allow our body to do? Our senses are gates into our spirit. We could be opening these gates (or doors) and giving place to the devil in ignorance. We must submit these areas to God but we must not *only* submit to God, we must also resist the devil if we expect to be delivered (James 4:7).

Satan can lure a child of God away from the truth, bind him or her up and weaken the individual to the point where he (the devil) can attach an unclean spirit. When this happens, the cure is to cast out the spirit. Prevention, however, is better than cure and this is why Christians are warned not to be ignorant (2 Corinthians 2:11). We are to put on the whole armor of God (Ephesians 6:11, 12). Remember, the devil is after us because he does not own us (1 Peter 5:8).

Our Eyes

We are warned in Scripture to set no evil thing before our eyes (Psalm 101:3). Whether it is pornographic and or suggestive pictures, advertising, movies, television, pornographic writing, horror pictures, degrading comic books, things mocking authority, or acts of violence, we are not to look at these things. All these, just to name a few, provoke our imaginations and open us and or our children to satanic bondages, which may result in many problems such as fantasies, rebelliousness, and lawlessness. Often we hear a person blaming God for temptations, reasoning it to be a test. Satan is the tempter, NOT God. God never tempts us (James 1:13-16).

We must believe that we will never be overcome by more temptation than we can withstand, but believe that God will make a way of escape (1 Corinthians 10:13). It is up to us, however, whether we choose to take the way of escape that God provides. When bad thoughts or ideas come because of our eyes, we must discipline ourselves to only watch pure things. If we refuse to take this action we open ourselves up to unclean spirits.

"My son, let thine eyes look right on" (Proverbs 4:25).

Our Ears

The Bible says

"My son, (and that includes daughters too), incline thine ear unto my sayings. They are life unto those that find them" (Proverbs 4:20-22).

We must not allow ourselves to hear wrong words, unclean conversation, and stories with double meanings, vulgarities, dirty jokes, foolish talk, scary stories, and the satanic beat of hard rock music, etc., all of which put our carnal mind and imaginations to work and open the door to unclean spirits.

Our Mind

Our mind can be compared to a computer that is constantly feeding instructions to our body. We must decide who writes the programs for our computer. Will it be God, or Satan? The Bible says, *"If there be any virtue and if there be any praise, think on these things"* (Philippians 4:8).

Why? To keep the door closed.

If our thought lives are under attack by things such as

daydreaming, fantasies, mind relaxation methods, yoga, Transcendental Meditation, meditating on the wrong things, levitation, hypnosis, and various other New Age practices, they must never be given in to if we are to keep on the whole armor of God. An undisciplined mind invites anxiety and anxiety attacks (Isaiah 26:3).

Even our attitudes are often under attack. A poor attitude toward God invites demon oppression (Romans 1:31, 32). For example, the wrong attitude on giving invites poverty (Deuteronomy 28:47, 48). Disrespect for ones parents invites curses during our lifetime and the possibility of an early death (Ephesians 6:2, 3).

To reverse these curses ungodly attitudes must be renounced and replaced with the truth of God's Word. Having the attitude of doing everything as unto God makes life easier (Colossians 3:23) and brings that inner joy which is our strength (Nehemiah 8:10). When we feel as though our life is missing peace and inner joy, it is because our mind is not stayed on Jesus (Isaiah 26:3). When our mind is stayed on Him, the door to the devil gets closed. However, it may be necessary to cast down thoughts, temptations and wrong attitudes several times before we get the victory. *"And let us not be weary in well-doing; for in due season we shall reap, if we faint not"* (Galatians 6:9).

Sinning With Our Body

A Holy Body

Once we have received Christ, our body no longer belongs to us or to the devil. It belongs to God, and as His children we are charged with the responsibility of keeping it in acceptable condition. We must only allow our body to perform acceptable acts (1 Corinthians 6:19, 20). If we were not taught discipline by our parents as children we must ask the Lord for help in learning to discipline ourselves as adults. If we refuse to discipline our body, we can open the door to the devil.

Holiness is our reasonable service to God (Romans 12:1, 2). Without holiness we will not see God and without deliverance we will not see holiness (Hebrews 12:14). God does not ask us to do something that is impossible, holiness is attainable and is expected of us by God. We are willing bondservants to Jesus, not slaves to Satan.

Holiness has a purpose. It is a part of our armor that protects us from Satan and his unclean spirits. Misconduct with our body gives place to the devil and is disobedience to God's word. It can bring the child of God under the control of evil spirits. When we are undisciplined and give in to the lusts of the flesh God is not given His proper place and we are drawn deeper into sin. Lack of discipline invites the powers of darkness to come upon us (Romans 1:21-28).

Common Areas of Temptation

Satan is clever. He may not be able to entice us into vulgar sins, but he has little trouble luring us into committing more subtle ones. Perhaps he may not be able to get us to take a cocktail or a can of beer, but he has no problem getting us to overeat. There is much preaching about drunkenness, drug abuse and smoking, but little about gluttony among Christians. There are several very subtle but common areas where we can open the door to the devil without even realizing that we have done so. We can, with the following list, take an inventory to see where we may be missing the mark:

- Excessive eating can result in receiving a spirit of gluttony.

- Sex before marriage invites a spirit of fornication (1 Corinthians 6:9), not to mention the possibility of illegitimate children and sexually transmitted diseases including AIDS.

- Sex outside of marriage invites a spirit of fornication and adultery (1 Corinthians 6:9), illegitimate children and sexually transmitted diseases including AIDS. Adultery can destroy our soul (Proverbs 6:32).

- Masturbation is sex with self, not the marriage partner, and invites a perverted spirit and other unclean spirits (2 Timothy 3:2; 1 Corinthians 6:9).

- Smoking, whether it is drugs of some sort, cigarettes or cigars (or using tobacco in any other way) destroys our body and invites, not only lung cancer and cancer of the throat, mouth, and larynx, but many other diseases as well (1 Corinthians 6:19, 20).

- Using drugs, even prescription drugs, indiscriminately, opens the door to addictions and witchcraft (1 Corinthians 6:19, 20; Revelation 18:23).

- Gambling, including the Lottery (the tax on the willing) invites a spirit of poverty and addiction. We are not to be brought under the power of anything (1 Corinthians 6:12).

- Other acts of perversion such as transvestitism, and transgender behaviors invite homosexual spirits (Romans 1:26).

- Bestiality invites an animal spirit and great confusion (Leviticus 18:23).

- Drunkenness invites depression and addiction (Galatians 5:21, 6:8). It ruins one's health and brings pain and misery to families.

Addiction to Drugs

Drug addiction is running rampant in the world today. It is a battle for the body, mind and soul. Casual use is most likely caused by the lust of the flesh, however, with constant casual recreational use a person can eventually become addicted and a slave to the substance. It is at this point that the person has taken in a demon spirit. This is true, not just for drugs, but in every area that defiles, enslaves and torments. Read 1 Corinthians 6:12. We can be taken over, so be wise, and avoid exposure. Drug addiction separates the conscious mind from the subconscious, allowing demons to enter the subconscious mind, destroying Christian values and attitudes previously established in a person's life.

In deliverance counseling it has been discovered that addiction to various drugs can invite visitation by evil supernatural spirits. Tobacco use invites nicotine drug spirits. Nicotine has been found to be more addictive than cocaine. We would not smoke in Church, then why would we want to pollute our bodies with all the dangerous chemicals contained in smoke? Our body is the Temple of the Holy Spirit (1 Corinthians 6:19, 20).

Addiction to Alcohol

Every addiction is driven by Satan. He loves to get persons addicted to anything, physical or mental, for then that person is taken away from God's ideal of control over the physical body and mind through the power of the Holy Spirit. God wants us to be in control of our bodies and minds. Satan wants that control to be shifted to him through any means possible, including alcohol. Countless lives have been lost over the centuries to the demon of drinking. Liver disease and brain damage, just to name a few, are conditions that occur from years of drinking alcohol and drunk drivers kill thousands of innocent victims on our roadways.

Piercing and Tattooing

One of the signs of a society slipping into Satanism is a surge in the tribal mentality phenomenon of body piercing and tattoos. God forbade tattooing of the body in Deuteronomy 14:1 and Leviticus 19:28 because it was a pagan and uncivilized practice used in the worship of false gods.

Sexuality Can Be Distorted By the Enemy

The church has failed miserably to teach sexual ethics in a positive and helpful way to our succeeding generations of young people. The Bible is not coy and prudish when it comes to sexuality. In many places it is very explicit in its descriptions but it is very clear that sex is intended only within the covenant of marriage.

Reproduction for mankind was a supreme part of God's creative act in making men and women. In it he chose not only to share his creative power but to give man something unknown to the rest of creation. Only man, not any other creature, is described to have been made in the image of God. We have the ability to know each other in the spirit as well as experience each other with the emotions and be connected by way of the sexual organs – in the flesh.

Since sex is a spiritual matter, it is critical to understand the ways Satan tries to pervert sexuality to destroy its spiritual dimension, which gives Christian sex inside marriage such wonderful potential. Because of ignorance of God's plan for sex many Christians' sexual relationships fall very short of God's intention.

Sex was intended for marriage and most people do not realize they are opening themselves up to demonic affliction by engaging in illicit sex outside of marriage. Our society has become so saturated with the tremendous media hype of sex with anyone at any time, for any reason – that tens of millions of people have opened wide that spiritual doorway not only to themselves but to their children as well.

Most TV sitcoms these days, and most movies, TV shows, and novels depict unbiblical sex. Even though God is not going to allow Himself to be mocked forever (Galatians 6:7), Satan is having a field day right now! His demonic hosts are striding through the spiritual doorways opened in the hearts of so many today to afflict them in every way.

Every time a person has sex outside of marriage an ungodly soul-tie is established and the demons are given the right to enter. It is important to explore areas of previous sexual relationships, especially with people who appear to have been suffering for some time with problems (medical or otherwise) that may have persisted without apparent reason or which have been undiagnosed. It is not unusual to find that spirits of infirmity (often times sexual spirits will lodge in the lower back) or of the occult (causing oppression) have taken advantage of an ungodly soul-tie and transferred from one sex partner to the other. Giving in to unnatural sex urges, including Internet pornography sites will invite spirits of incest, pornography, prostitution, homosexuality, pedophilia, etc.

God designed man and woman to have intercourse by the insertion of the male sexual organ into the female one. Ejaculation of the male sperm into the female is the means of fertilizing ovum so that reproduction may occur. Ejaculation into any other orifice of the body is a perversion of what God planned and purposed for mankind. When people, married or not, indulge in such perverted sex, demons with perverted character can enter. The consequences can be anything from physical infirmities to increasingly lustful desire for more perverted sex. Both oral and anal are major demonic entry points (Horrobin 138-139).

Homosexuality and Lesbianism

The homosexual lifestyle is expressly forbidden in Scripture. There are several references in both the Old and the New Testaments (Leviticus 18:11, Romans 1:26-32). There is no other way to interpret these passages than literally. Social and cultural changes will not change the Word of God to mean anything else when in the eyes of God homosexuality and lesbianism is wrong.

Indulgence in homosexual relationships of any type provides a wide open door for the enemy to come in like a flood. It is rare to find someone who has either been the victim of homosexual abuse, or someone who has willingly, even in ignorance, had such contact with people, who is not demonized and in need of deliverance.

There are many potential causes of homosexuality, but in all cases the option of condoning the sin on the grounds that the person did not choose the lifestyle avoids the issue of a spiritual source being at the root of the tendency. Having tendencies is not a sin if the person remains celibate; however, if the person is promiscuous, as many homosexuals and lesbians are, promiscuity in itself is sinful whether it is homosexual or heterosexual. God has ordained marriage to be between a man and a woman only, therefore, it is impossible for two men or two women to be married to one another. Thus, every homosexual and or lesbian act is fornication in the eyes of God.

Possible Causes of Homosexual Tendencies May Include

- A generational spirit of homosexuality that is passed down through a parent. This could come from the parents themselves or from much further back in the generational line.

- Rejection of the gender of a child instilling the message in the spirit that he or she is the wrong sex. Sexual expectations of the parents will inevitably affect the spirit of the baby. The child may subconsciously try to live up to the sexual expectations of the parents and perform as the opposite sex of what they actually are. Rejection by parents is fertile ground for the demonic and will form an open door for a spirit of homosexuality to enter the developing child.

- Homosexual sexual abuse is perhaps the most common source of homosexual demonization. Not uncommonly, it can even enter through children abusing one another, especially if there is a generational spirit of homosexuality in one of the children. Conversely, it is very uncommon to hear of a homosexual person or pedophile that was not molested at some point in his or her life, usually as a child.

- Willing homosexual relationships that are entered into by people, and often curious teenagers, who have no previous background of homosexual relationships, either personally or generationally. In today's "anything goes" mentality, people are willing to try anything new and different just for the perceived thrill. If and when the person discovers this lifestyle is not for him or her it may be too late since the demonic spirits may have already entered. If they are not allowed by the person to manifest by performing perverted sex acts, they will manifest in any way they can to confuse, torment and oppress.

- Pornography used for obtaining illegitimate sexual pleasure, can be the source of extensive demonization. We live in an age when pictures of the naked body, especially of women, are displayed daily in front of our eyes, however, simply noticing images of nudity, is different from using pornography viewed in a deliberate way.

The Word tells us that we are to be in the world but not of the world (John 15:19, 17:1-26). In view of this, there must be a way through the overt sexual jungle of the world, enabling us to live in the midst of such things without entering into personal sin where the demonic is given a right of entry.

The Consequences

The consequences of all wrongful sex, whether willingly or unwillingly entered into, are more extensive than just demonization. All aspects of the damage need to be ministered to in order to bring healing to the person. Casting out the demons is essential, but our job as deliverance counselors is to bring healing to people. The many layers of problems caused in a life through many years of being demonized requires careful, thorough, and loving ministry.

Other Areas of Sexual Involvement

There are various other areas of involvement as well that can open doors to the evil supernatural that can result in oppression and torment. In recent years we have seen an exponential increase in the following areas of deception. Persons who have been involved in abortion, whether mothers, fathers, doctors, nurses, or any other participants, will need to be delivered from spirits of murder and death and sometimes spirits of grief, anxiety, insanity and guilt.

Immodest dress and exposure, for women, men, children and teenagers will invite a provocative spirit, a harlot spirit, a whore or for men, a whore mongering spirit. Worst of all, a spirit of rape can enter causing the person to be repeatedly attacked or molested. God does not want us to expose ourselves or our children to any of these kinds of attacks.

We Can Resist

In 1 Corinthians 10:13 we are told quite clearly that we are absolutely able to escape temptation.

"Wherefore let him that thinketh he standeth take heed lest he fall. There hath no temptation taken you but such as is common to man; but God is faithful, who will not suffer you to be tempted above that ye are able; but will with the

temptation also make a way to escape, that ye may be able to bear it" (1 Corinthians 10: 12, 13).

Just because we might slip and fall does not mean that we have taken in an unclean spirit, but it does mean that we have opened the door and that door must be closed.

Jesus warns us in Matthew 7:24-27 that Christians can expect the storm to hit like a hurricane. Our triune house needs to be strong enough to resist and endure. It must be understood that it is not a sin to be tempted but we must determine to take the way of escape. The problem with unclean spirits comes if we have built our house on sand (Matthew 7:26). God says we are to *submit* and resist (James 4:7).

Ministering Hope

Some counselees will feel as though there is no hope for them because they have done things with their mind and body that are so reprehensible they could never be forgiven. They may feel they have invited so many problems that they could never get free. What then is the answer for them? In the eyes of God it is impossible to be too far gone to get free. With the help of the Lord it is possible to obtain forgiveness and deliverance from every kind of demonic torment. But there is a process that the counselee must follow:

- First, he or she must submit wholly to God, and resist the devil (James 4:7).

- He or she must call upon the Lord. Joel 2:32 tells us that "ALL who call upon the Lord shall be delivered."

- The Apostle Paul said to the new Christians in Corinth, "... and such were some of you." but NOW they werewashed, sanctified, justified and set free (1 Corinthians 6:11).

- Then, in order to close all the doors, claim God's promise for the situation and cast the devils out, one by one, in the Name of Jesus.

Witchcraft and the Occult

What are Witchcraft and the Occult?

Witchcraft and occult activities involve seeking supernatural guidance or help by some means other than going to God through the Blood of Jesus Christ. The First Commandment says that HE is the Lord our God, and we are not to have any other gods before Him (Exodus 20:2-5). Witchcraft is spiritual adultery (Ezekiel 23:37).

God and Satan are the only sources of power, hidden information, guidance, healing, knowledge, and supernatural help. Since man is created for worship, he will either worship Christ or Satan. Since many do not know that there are not one, but two sources of the supernatural, they are easily deceived. The Bible clearly shows the two sources of supernatural power. In Exodus 7:8-13 we see that Godly and satanic supernatural power is nothing new, and they are both very real. However real Satan's power may be, God's power is shown to be far more superior (Exodus 8:16:19). We must choose which source we will seek, we cannot have both. We cannot serve God and Satan (Joshua 24:15).

Good Witches and Bad Witches

The form of witchcraft called WICCA, presents itself to be "white witchcraft." Wiccan "white witches" are deceived into thinking they are good witches, involved in doing exploits for God. We must not be fooled, ALL witchcraft is evil! SATANISM, however, makes no such claims. It is all out black witchcraft and its followers actually worship Satan and, in some cases, go so far as to engage in blood sacrifices and pray fervently against Christians and especially our leaders.

Wiccans worship in the nude. They refer to this practice as being "sky clad." Some give up their virgin daughters to the male leaders for perverted sexual acts. These are only a few of their "good witch" practices.

Often it is those whose lives have left them feeling helpless and out of control and teenagers who feel disenfranchised. These people who have the feeling of powerlessness are often fascinated by and are drawn into witchcraft and the occult because it promises supernatural control and power. Listed below are some of the warning signs that a person might be involved:

- Having in their possession books on the occult, witchcraft or Satanism, particularly the satanic bible or a book of satanic rituals.

- Having in their possession heavy metal albums or gangster rap by groups who promote and practice Satanism or the occult.

- Owning and wearing clothing with occult or satanic symbols appearing on it. Or having in their possession books, drawings or tattoos with occult symbols.

- Occult tattoos or an unusual amount of tattoos and piercings.

- A fascination with weapons, murder, suicide or death in general.

- Having in their possession occult computer games and/or videos.

- Dressing in all black, "Gothic" type clothing and makeup. Teens who are involved even call themselves "Goths." They are involved in witchcraft and are embracing, romancing and celebrating witchcraft and death whether they know it or not.

- The dictionary defines Gothic as barbaric, uncouth and uncivilized.

Ignorance Is No Excuse

Just as ignorance is no excuse when it comes to civil law, ignorance is no excuse when it comes to spiritual law. Isaiah 5:13 and Hosea 4:6 both state very clearly that we can go into bondage and even be destroyed if we lack knowledge of Satan's devices or of the authority we have in Christ. Ignorance and gross disobedience are Satan's weapons against a child of God. In Isaiah the ignorance was the fault of the people themselves, in Hosea the ignorance came because of wrong teaching. Many born-again believers are being disobedient to God and are actually practicing witchcraft whether they realize it or not. Some of the ways they can become involved are:

- By reading horoscopes, even if one does not "believe in them."

- By going to psychic readers or fortune tellers.

- By watching television programs containing witchcraft and magic themes.

- By watching television programs or movies about ghosts, which are demon spirits.

- By wearing demonic charms, ankhs, horns, etc., believed to have supernatural power over natural forces. Anything that is worn to ward off evil spirits actually attracts them.

- By wearing Zodiac jewelry and jewelry associated with secret societies.

- By going to New Age healers and using some of

the "alternative medicine" treatments that have their roots in occult practices.

- By using illegal drugs or by abusing prescription drugs.

- By listening to "heavy metal" rock and gangster rap music and attending rock concerts.

Discerning of Spirits

The Bible clearly shows that Satan will try to seduce us so that we miss God's will and drive us on to despair and destruction (1Timothy 4:1). He will try to weaken us to where he can attach an unclean spirit to us to control our life. When the spirit gets control, the unbeliever and believer alike will need to seek help, he or she will need deliverance! God knew we would need supernatural help to discern between good and evil because it is a very subtle "fine line." This is why we have available to us the gift of discerning of spirits (1 Corinthians 12:10).

Unfortunately many have unteachable attitudes and are deceived because they lack knowledge of God's Word, lack discernment or because they choose to believe a lie or a false doctrine. Look at the fruit that is produced by these practices. We can know whether or not they are from God by their fruit (1 John 4:1-3).

Common Areas of Involvement

All of the following areas of involvement are dangerous

and can cause demon activity and demonic visitation to occur.

- Tea leaf or palm reading, fortunetellers and "readers," psychics, crystal balls, reincarnation and water witching.

- Ouija boards, tarot cards, occult toys, occult computer games, videos and television shows.

- Table or chair lifting, Mary Worth games (usually played at pre-teen sleepovers).

- Mental telepathy, extrasensory perception or ESP. In actuality those initials should stand for evil spirit power.

- Handwriting analysis (not the forensic type), astrology or horoscopes, voodoo, Santeria, clairvoyance, levitation, hypnotism, or channeling at séances, ghost chasing.

- Cabala, praying to saints, automatic handwriting, pendulums, yoga, karate or other martial arts.

- Transcendental Meditation classes, hard rock, heavy metal or gangster rap music concerts.

- Horror movies with extreme violence and acts of torture and murder.

- Reading or practicing the teachings of Edgar Cayce, Jean Dixon, Unity, Nostradamus, Albert Ford, Ruth

Montgomery, the Rosicrucian's, Mormonism (the Church of Latter Day Saints, which teaches "another" Jesus). Unitarianism, Jehovah's Witnesses, Baha'i, Theosophy, Christian Science (which isn't really Christian at all). Metaphysics, Freemasonry and or Scientology, just to name a few.

Not All Satanic Things Are Vulgar

Make no mistake about it, all of the above are satanic and involvement in them is an open invitation for demonic visitation and harassment, but not all satanic things are vulgar. In fact, they can be very inviting and interesting. That is why many well-meaning people are innocently deceived as religious demons manifest as angels of light (2 Corinthians 11:14-15). We must take back this ground to insure that we will be able to retain our deliverance. It is necessary to burn or otherwise destroy, everything that pertains to these false religions (Acts 19:19-20). We must not arbitrarily begin to dispose of things or counsel anyone to do so, but rather pray with counselees and explain to them that the Holy Spirit will reveal what needs to go.

Music, Dancing and Drugs

Believers in Bible times used music and dancing to worship and praise God. Like the believers of old, we too give God the sacrifice of praise willingly and from our hearts with music and dancing before Him. Satan's desire, however, is to counterfeit God, therefore the music and dancing that he requires, as his worship is evil and sensual.

Satan uses evil music to pervert human emotions and command praise and worship from his followers. The combination of Rock music, alcohol and drugs is especially insidious and has a narcotic effect. It causes irrational behavior in our youth and altered states of consciousness, sometimes to the point of causing them to commit rape, murder and suicide. The new, designer drugs that are coming onto the scene are lethal and can cause permanent brain damage (Ecstasy and Methamphetamine for instance), and must never be ingested, smoked, or injected.

Witchcraft and Our Children

Literature that involved witchcraft was very difficult to find several years ago. Now, however, it is not just creeping into, but flooding into, not only adult literature, but into our children's literature as well. The Harry Potter series of books are a good example. These books actually teach children to cast spells and curses on those they dislike and are blatantly teaching our children against the teachings of Jesus Christ and the Bible. These types of literature, and the movies made from them, are extremely dangerous.

Ways We Can Be Unknowingly Involved In Witchcraft

- Using our eyes to control, dominate or manipulate another person. (Mark 7:21-22).

- Stubbornness and rebellion often result from occult involvement (1 Samuel 15:23).

- Don't be fooled into believing that there are "good" witches, all witchcraft is bad and abominable to God (Deuteronomy 18:12).

- Even if these things were done prior to salvation does not mean that they do not need to be dealt with. God has forgiven and forgotten, but Satan has not! We still reap what we sow in this life (Galatians 6:7). For example: An unmarried girl may get pregnant and then get saved. God forgives her the fornication and the illegitimate pregnancy when she gets saved, but she will still be pregnant and have the baby.

Common Results of Witchcraft and Occult Involvement

There are common resultant manifestations of being involved in witchcraft or the occult. The following is a list of some of the manifestations, but not all of them.

- Seeing apparitions or ghosts and or being visited by poltergeists, which are noisy spirits who often move things around to bring fear and confusion.

- Being visited by incubus spirits during the night (sex spirits manifesting as males), or succubus spirits (sex spirits manifesting as females) sometimes resulting in orgasm.

- Having nightmares and the feeling of being "held down" or "paralyzed" during the night. In these instances the Blood of Jesus must be pled, even in a sound sleep because the spirit never sleeps and is fully capable of commanding these demons to leave

- Strange physical sensations, such as vibrating, and severe heart palpitations.

- Confusion and feelings of going insane.

- Perverted sex desires (remember, witchcraft is spiritual fornication).

- Hearing voices that sometimes threaten harm if their wishes are not carried out and those wishes can be murder and or suicide. These voices must be countered by refusing to listen to them and by pleading the blood of Jesus over the mind and thoughts

Depression, Despondency, and Suicide

Although these symptoms can be brought about by other causes, such as chemical imbalances in the brain, it is important to discover if the person, (or others in the family), have been involved in witchcraft or the occult. Many times the tormented person hears demonic voices telling them to commit suicide. These suicide spirits can also be the cause of accidents. No one suspects that the evil spirit behind the accident is actually suicide because the accident hides their true nature. In view of that, be sure to come against a spirit of suicide if a person has had repeated accidents or if this is what the Holy Spirit reveals.

A tormented individual may think the voices are from his or her own thoughts or from God when in fact they are demon spirits attempting to destroy the person. These demon spirits must be cast out. However, the person being affected must be willing to renounce the voices and refuse to listen to them, and be willing to renounce the depression and ask God for forgiveness. Our bodies are the Temple of the Holy Spirit and we are not to destroy it (1 Corinthians 6:19).

Consequences of Witchcraft and Occult Experimentation

God warns us in His Word not to get involved in certain practices. When God gives a warning, it is not to deprive us from having fun; it is to keep us from being destroyed. Some of those warnings include:

- Do not get involved in the first place (Deuteronomy 18:9-12).

- It is possible for a person to lose his or her sanity (Isaiah 8:19-22) or be destroyed (Isaiah 47:11-14).

- We can lose our life (1 Chronicles 10:13, 14) and we may end up in hell (Revelation 21:8).

What Are We To Do If We Have Already Been Involved?

It is imperative that anyone who has been involved destroy everything in his or her possession that is in any way connected with an occult practice. We cannot just give these things away to someone else as these items could destroy that person as well.

- Destroy books and symbols of demon power (Acts 19:19-20; Deuteronomy 7:25, 26). They are not harmless trinkets, toys, or study tools; but invitations for demon visitation.
- Destroy garments that may have been worn during demon worship or in any other unclean act (Jude 23).

- Destroy carved heads, masks, Buddha statues and witchcraft objects. Christians can have problems because of seemingly harmless objects and mementos brought home from missionary trips.

- Destroy rock and gangster rap music and or movies.

When we destroy these things, the Holy Spirit will be free to move. If we keep them, we are being disobedient to God and encouraging the demons to keep us company. Destroying these objects will close the doors to the evil supernatural. At that time implement this five-step procedure, which is a spiritual legal transaction, with the counselee showing him or her that it is necessary to: 1) Recognize that the problem is demonic. The Holy Spirit will help when we pray. 2) Repent and be willing to turn away from these things for good. 3) Renounce and "take back" the ground given to the devil. 4) Ask forgiveness of God and forgiveness of persons from former generations who may have initiated the witchcraft in the family.5) Cast out the demons and thank God for freedom at last.

With occult involvement it is possible for the victim to actually "befriend" these demons. God will not deliver anyone from his or her friends if there is a desire to keep them. It is possible for a person to have become so involved in friendship with demonic spirits that it will take a strong commitment and a concerted effort for him or her to discontinue listening to the voices and choose human friends once again.

The New Age Movement Religion

What is The New Age Movement?

The New Age Movement (NAM) is a title that refers to a world view or philosophy of life that many people hold. The NAM can also be called a religion because it is based on religious views. In the 1960's and 1970's New Agers were telling us that a new age was dawning. Astrologers called it the Age of Aquarius. Even in the face of perplexing world conditions the New Agers expected there to be a quantum leap into a new global era of peace, harmony and truth. (Ankerberg/Weldon (7).

World Peace or the Prince of Peace?

The Bible also heralds the coming of a new world order, but what it says about how it will arrive and what kind of world it will be differs radically from the New Age

Movement's teachings. When the Bible refers to Jesus as the Prince of Peace (Isaiah 9:6) it is not referring to Him having brought, or bringing in the future, peace on earth. Contrary to the New Age thought, there will never be peace on earth until God has set up His Kingdom in the New Jerusalem. The peace that Jesus came to bring is peace between man and his God. Hope in God's reign, not in evolution, fills the Christian's vision and the culmination of history will not be some great planetary consciousness but it will be the return of the Lord Jesus Christ for His Bride.

New Agers hold to pantheism, a belief that God is all, and all is God, and that every person is a part of God (Ankerberg/Weldon 7). The Bible teaches we are not God, but God's. We are created in His image (Genesis 1:27). Through mystical experiences, and altered states of consciousness, people are persuaded that the religion of the New Age is true. Actually, extrasensory knowledge, channeling spirit guides, (the Bible calls it sorcery and an abomination to God) and out of body experiences are given by demons to deceive individuals into believing the New Age lies.

New Agers believe God to be energy, "the force" as in the film Star Wars. The Bible tells us that God is not an impersonal force, energy, or higher power, as in the 12 step self-help programs. He is not just a consciousness; He is a living, personal being.

The New Age "truth" is the old witchcraft lie. We cannot find life and salvation within ourselves, apart from the one true God. This was the serpent's temptation in the garden (Genesis 3) and his strategies haven't changed much.

God's Word warns that in the latter times some shall

depart from the faith, giving heed to seducing spirits and doctrines of devils (1 Timothy 4:1). The devil is a liar and the father of lies (John 8:44). Demons masquerade as guardian angels, angels of light and friendly spirit guides (2 Corinthians 11:14). New Agers teach that evil is an illusion and belief in an absolute morality is wrong. The New Age Movement is extremely dangerous because it is shifting the way Americans think away from Christian values to the practices of witchcraft. The New Age thought has permeated our schools, our colleges, classrooms, and our boardrooms.

Ignorance

In the instance of the New Age teachings, as it is concerning witchcraft and the occult, Biblical ignorance and worldliness are not valid excuses (Isaiah 5:13; Hosea 4:6). Many born again believers are being disobedient to God and are actually getting involved in New Age practices, some of which are even purported to be Christian. These involvements include:

- Transcendental Meditation and Yoga.

- Various "holistic" therapies such as acupuncture, acupressure, homeopathy, iridology, reflexology, biofeedback, etc.

- Reading books written by spirits, produced by automatic writing by mediums (sometimes called channelers).

Be advised – most of the books found in the Occult section of bookstores and libraries were inspired by demons. Some have even been best sellers. Every book that purports to give instructions on how to communicate with angels is definitely demonic. God's angels will not communicate with humans but Satan's hoard would love to get hold of our minds in this way for the purpose of evil. The most obvious reason for Christian acceptance of such material is the fact that biblical ignorance and worldliness are common among Christians. The Church is failing to educate people properly in these areas, but that is why God has given us the gift of discerning of spirits (1 Corinthians 12:10).

Common Areas of Involvement

- Channeling and calling up spirits of the dead.

- Communicating with angels.

- Astral projection and out of body experiences.

- Eckancar, which is a cult that engages in astral projection (soul travel).

- All Eastern religions.

- Fortune telling of every sort including Tarot Cards.

- Scientific mysticism and the paranormal including UFO obsession.

- Scientology and Dianetics

- Mind sciences, crystals.

- Transcendental Meditation and mantras.

- Any practices, including drugs that cause altered states of consciousness.

- Reincarnation teachings and Karma. Hebrews 9:27 tells us:

"And as it is appointed unto man once to die, but after this the judgment."

Many Holistic Health Practices are Related to the New Age Movement

The holistic health movement is the "medical arm" of the New Age and includes a variety of unsound practices:

- Applied Kinesiology (muscle testing).

- Homeopathy (a diluting of certain essences for medical treatment).

- Iridology (the alleged medical diagnosis of diseases by inspection of the iris).

- Therapeutic Touch (an Eastern form of the laying on of hands).

- Herbal concoctions purporting to have phenomenal healing properties. Many of these come from the orient and contain very weird ingredients including animal parts.

- Any therapies that claim to manipulate "invisible energy."

- Hypnotism.

- Dozens of other, unproven treatments.

In New Age Medicine, authors Paul Reisser, MD, Terri Reisser, and John Weldon list the following important cautions about New Age Medical practices: beware of therapies which claim to manipulate "invisible energy"; beware of those who seem to utilize psychic knowledge or power; beware of a practitioner who has a therapy with which no one else is familiar; beware of someone who claims that his or her particular therapy will cure anything; beware of someone whose explanations do not make sense; beware of therapies whose only proof consists of the testimonies of satisfied customers; beware of therapies which rely heavily on altered states of consciousness; and finally realize that sincerity is no guarantee of legitimacy (Reisser/ Reisser/ Weldon 148-151). Most holistic therapies are unscientific in nature and as such are potentially dangerous in a case of life-threatening illness. Some treatments may even work because of the occult power behind them but in the end the person involved will be snared by the demons these practices carry with them.

The New Age Movement is related to certain "fringe"

psychotherapies. An example of which might be the new methods being used to bring to the surface "repressed, forgotten memories." These counseling methods are also related to witchcraft and hypnotism. One of the ways in which there is agreement among New Agers is the belief that "all is one, all is God and we are our own gods." New Agers teach:

- Faith in God is unnecessary (see Hebrews 11:1).

- Christ is man's "higher self" (see John 3:16-18; Philippians 2:1-9).

- Death is absolutely safe, merely a change without judgment (see John 3:36; Hebrews 9:27, Revelation 20:10-15).

- All is one; there is no good or evil (see Genesis 3:5).

- We will obtain cosmic evolution through reincarnation, one-worldism, and through contact with alleged extraterrestrials (Hebrews 9:27).

Common Results of New Age Involvement

Make no mistake; the New Age religions are a form of the occult. There are common resultant manifestations of being involved with their teachings. Following are just a few examples:

- Seeing apparitions or ghosts.

- Being visited by demons who claim to be spirit guides, ascended masters, masters of light, spirits of former lives, guardian angels or spirits of dead relatives and friends.

- Night visits by incubus spirits (sex spirits manifesting as males), and succubus spirits (sex spirits manifesting as females).

- Nightmares included the paralyzing feeling of being held down or choked.

- Strange physical sensations.

- Hearing voices.

- Insanity and confusion.

- Delusions or feelings of being "called" or in some special way privy to the secrets of the universe.

Consequences of Involvement in New Age Mind Altering Practices

The Bible gives us many warnings and refers to teachings of the occult and the New Age Movement as witchcraft. God's Word says that witchcraft is not only displeasing to God, but is an abomination to Him. These things invite His judgment and demon spirit visitation.

New Agers have simply adopted new names for old witchcraft.

- What the Bible calls an observer of times or an enchanter, they call an astrologer.

- What the Bible calls a medium or a wizard, they call a channeler.

- What the Bible calls familiar spirits, the New Agers call spirit guides, ascended masters or guardian angels. There are guardian angels of course, but we are not to traffic (communicate) with them (Deuteronomy 18:9-14).

We are not to have any other god but the one true God. We are not to get involved. These practices are detestable to the Lord. We are not to have fellowship with or participate with demons in any way (1 Corinthians 10:20).

What are we to do if we Have Already Been Involved?

Any one of the above practices can be the cause of many of our problems. These lists are not exhaustive. There may be many other ways to become involved. The gift of discerning of spirits will again help to identify any other areas of involvement. As with witchcraft and occult items, the way to get free is to destroy all New Age literature and symbols as well (Acts 19:19, 20). When we destroy them, the Holy Spirit is free to move, but if we keep them in our possession, the devil will keep us in his. The door needs to be closed and the five-step procedure of recognizing, repenting, renouncing, forgiving, and casting out needs to be followed once again. Jesus told the infirm man that He healed at the pool of Bethesda,

"Behold, thou art made whole: sin no more, lest a worse thing come unto thee" (John 5:14).

Cults and Secret Societies

What are Cults and Secret Societies?

Webster's New World Dictionary defines a cult as a quasi-religious group, often living in a colony, with a captivating leader who indoctrinates members with unorthodox or extremist views, practices, or beliefs; a devoted attachment to, or extravagant admiration for, a person, principle or lifestyle."

Not all cults and secret societies are so easily identified however. Some of them not only profess to be Christian, but to the untrained observer, they even seem to be Christian but they are not. They carry the voices of false prophets and they are very dangerous.

The explosion of interest in psychic phenomena has been relatively recent. Who had heard of Scientology or TM thirty or forty years ago? The few religious groups in America that were labeled cults by the established churches were nearly all offshoots of Christianity. They included Jehovah's Witnesses, Mormons, the Worldwide Church of God, Christian Science, Science of Mind, Religious Science, Unity, and Spiritualism. There has always been some Eastern Religious influence in some of them, the newer cults, however, are much more blatant in their practices of Eastern Mysticism. The new cults sweeping the West have popularized vegetarianism, reincarnation, karma, yoga, the martial arts, holistic heath practices, and various drugs, just to name a few. These cults are all extremely deceptive and seductive and are luring many into their lies because many today have itching ears and desire only to have them tickled with what they want to hear, rather than what they need to hear.

The Bible tells us in 2 Timothy 4:3, 4:

"For the time will come when they will not endure sound doctrine; but after their own lusts they shall heap to themselves teachers having itching ears. And they shall turn away their ears from the truth, and shall be turned unto fables."

The "insignia" of many of these cults is that they are led by at least one false prophet whose teachings are believed to be as important as or even more important than God's Word. Every false prophet has opened himself at some point in his life to a spirit of error. Error is easy to detect in some false prophets, but others are not so obvious. It is Satan's clever purpose to deceive people into thinking his followers and Christ's are saying about the same things. However, every cult is actually an attempt to set up a "kingdom" that will rule the universe, whether through technology, mind power, or under a Messiah, the ultimate purpose is always the same – to establish man as God (Hunt 240). Usually, cults and secret societies can be identified by the way the leader claims to have received instructions and revelation from angels or some other type of supernatural being or beings such as ascended masters or masters of light. The Apostle Paul warns,

"But though we or an angel from heaven preach any other gospel unto you than that which we have preached unto you, let him be accursed (Galatians 1:8).

Many times false teachers can be spotted if they skip through the Bible and choose only those verses they like in order to prove some pet point. The leaders often quote Scripture but we must not allow ourselves be fooled by Scripture quoting cultists, even Satan quotes Scripture. The false prophet's use of Scripture will often be out of context or incomplete. Cult members may show up at the door quoting Scripture from an authentic appearing "Bible." But, the truth is that many verses may have been altered to suit their false teachings. They often claim to have spiritual understanding of deeper truths. This can be an attempt to promote false teaching. God does not call some of the Bible deep and some shallow. The entire Bible is the true, inspired Word of God (2 Timothy 3:16).

Often, cult members will separate themselves and draw followers away from families so as to control their minds. The followers often lose the ability to make even the most insignificant decisions without the help of the leader. Many believe they have been uniquely chosen as watchmen of some special knowledge until the appropriate time when God will reveal this truth to the masses through them. They often hold many in slavery with a false hope of spiritual advancement and salvation, which emphatically excludes the true Savior and Lord, Jesus Christ. Make no mistake about it, these false prophets and teachers are operating with the help of familiar spirits.

Transcendental Meditation

Whenever a person is taught to go into occult mediation and to deliberately clear their mind to it, they have opened a very large spiritual doorway into which any number and manner of demons can enter. While in this altered state of mind people will meet demons masquerading as other people, including Jesus Christ. Evil spirits may not be encountered for some time allowing for the person to become deeply involved with demons calling themselves friendly spirit guides, angels of light or masters of light (2 Corinthians 11:14). Millions have been deceived in this way and are eventually viciously attacked mentally, physically or both.

False Religions

Those who practice various forms of Eastern Mysticism, including Hinduism, Shintoism, Buddhism, and Islam along with thousands of other entire populations of India, Pakistan, China, and many other countries practicing occult based religions have known only human misery, poverty, and repression. These countries have long had a very low opinion of the worth of human life. Yet, today, New Age adherents cannot get enough of this type of religion.

Freemasonry

Freemasonry claims to be based upon the Bible, but is a mysterious system for earning one's own salvation, which directly opposes the biblical concept of grace. A Mason cherishes the hope that so long as he believes in some supreme being, whether it is Allah, Brahman, Buddha, a cosmic force, or whatever, and is faithful to Freemasonry, he will be accepted into the eternal kingdom of the Grand Lodge above. If being "guided by Masonry" is the way to gain admission into the Celestial Lodge above, as they believe, then why are they so secretive about Masonry? Should not everyone have an equal opportunity to learn how to reach that Grand Lodge? Jesus sent His disciples out to share the good news of a full and free salvation for all.

Ignorance

Ignorance of what the Bible really says, is no excuse (Isaiah 5:13; Hosea 4:6). Many born again believers are being disobedient to God and are actually getting involved in cults and secret societies. Don't be deceived. Although they may seem to be saying the same things the true followers of Christ are saying – when their teachings are held up to the light of the Bible, it is obvious they are not.

Discerning of Spirits

As in all the other ways in which we become involved in the evil supernatural, God will give us supernatural help to discern between good and evil. We can try the spirits; we can test them and know them by their fruit (1 John 4:1-3).

Common Areas of Involvement

Common areas of involvement in occult religious groups and secret societies are: Christian Science, Jean Dixon, Christadelphianism, Jesus Only, Confucianism, Edgar Cayce, Scientology, Hare Krishna, Mind Science, Hinduism, Rosicrucianism, I Ching, The Way International, Inner Peace Movement, Zen, Islam or Mormonism and many others.

Freemasonry, Red Cross of Constantine, Order of the Secret Monitor, Knights of Malta, Knights Templar, Masonic Royal Order of Scotland, Scottish Rite, Black Watch, Prince Hall Freemasonry, The Order of Amaranth, Royal Order of Jesters, Manchester Unity Order of Oddfellows, Elks, Moose, Eagles, Buffaloes, Druids, Grange, Orange Foresters.

Ku Klux Klan, Woodsmen of The World, Riders of the Red Robe, Knights of Pythias, Mystic Order of The Veiled Prophets of the Enchanted Realm, Order of Eastern Star, Ladies Oriental Shrine, White Shrine of Jerusalem, Daughters of Eastern Star, International Order of Job's Daughters, Rainbow Girls or the Order of De Molay and many others.

Common Results of Cult and Secret Society Involvement

There are common resultant manifestations of being a member of cults and or secret societies, the worst of which is that it is very difficult to come out of them. Adherents to cultic teachings are vulnerable to many torments yet they often remain insulated against the gospel with lies and are very difficult to bring to Christ. Some of these manifestations include:

- Fears imposed on Masons and other secret brotherhoods should they reveal the secrets.

- Men become "married" to their brotherhood and are in effect committing spiritual adultery. The true and open union of a couple in a marriage is prevented because of secrets that members dare not share with their wives. They are also committing spiritual adultery by placing every god on the level with the one true God (Hosea 4:12; John 17:3).

- Eyesight confusion and fears caused by blindfolded initiations can occur. Heart attacks, fear of heart attacks, chest pains and death from oaths taken during initiation for the heart to be ripped out should secrets be revealed.

- Insanity, a curse imposed by God on those involved in idolatry (Deuteronomy 28).

- Secretiveness which leads to inability to communicate effectively and which ruins many marriages.

Consequences of Involvement and Membership in Cults and Secret Societies

There are many warnings in God's Word against these

types of involvements. Do not get involved (Deuteronomy 18:9-12), one can go insane (Isaiah 8:19-22), one can be destroyed (Isaiah 47:11-14), one can lose his or her life (1 Chronicles 10:13, 14), and his or her eternity (Revelation 21:8).

What Am I to Do If I Am Involved or Have Become a Member?

Destroy all books and symbols of cults and or secret societies (Acts 19:19, 20; Deuteronomy 7:25, 26). They are not harmless study literature and objects; they are invitations for demon bondage and visitation. When we destroy them, the Holy Spirit is free to move. If we keep them, we are being disobedient to God and this encourages demons to keep us company.

Membership in any of the above cults, secret societies, brotherhoods, or fraternal organizations, can be the cause of the problems being experienced. These organizations are all satanic. Close the door and again, follow the five-step procedure for deliverance.

Part III
The Counseling Session

Ministering to Children

Discipline Protects Them

Demons are able to attack children as well as adults, therefore, they also can be harassed, oppressed, and in need of deliverance. Children can also be delivered by the same procedures. The process is often much easier since the spirits have not been there very long and children are generally more willing to listen to adults. However, the exception would be children who have been exposed to demonic attack through severe circumstances such as trauma from accidents or abuse. Since the child may feel more secure with a parent, it is often best for the parent to be there and hold the child during the ministry.

Most children by the age of five or six can be given a simple explanation of what is going to take place before beginning ministry. They need to know that we are not talking to them but to the spirits, otherwise they may be frightened by words of command addressed to the evil spirits.

Explain to the child that sometimes ugly things called bad spirits can tempt a boy or girl and cause them to do bad things they don't want to do and that it may be these bad spirits getting them into trouble and that the ugly spirits will be told to get away.

If the child has been having nightmares, which is a form of oppression that children often suffer, explain to the child that ugly monsters have been chased away taking the bad dreams with them. Explain to them that Jesus is their friend and Jesus is stronger than the monsters. Tell them that there is nothing to fear anymore and that they can even help to chase them away. Children will often understand and become cooperative.

Always remember, especially with children, that it is not the loudness of a command that moves the demon but the authority of the name and the blood of the Lord Jesus Christ. The commands can be given with such calmness that the child may scarcely realize what is taking place. Then teach the child that he or she can also chase the dream monsters away with the name of Jesus. (It is wise to use the same kind of language as the child).

Children are not competent to protect themselves and stay free once they are delivered; it is the responsibility of the parents or guardians. Parents are to consistently discipline their children in order to protect them. Parents are required to live the Christian life as examples to the children, instructing and relating family rules to the Bible, appropriating and implementing biblical values. Older children should be encouraged to read the book of Proverbs often.

Parental authority represents God to the child. If the child does not learn to respect their parents, he or she will have a very difficult time later on in life respecting the law of the land and the authority of God.

Abuse and Trauma

Unclean spirits can enter children several ways and by several kinds of circumstances. This often includes some type of abuse or trauma, by inheritance and or by sin. The abuse of children abounds in our world, physical, sexual and emotional.

Wherever there has been sexual abuse in a child's life, it is likely that demonization has taken place. These demons will seek to distort damage and destroy Godly relationships later in the child's adult life. When pedophile and perverted demons enter the child they usually do not leave them. For example, a girl may have been sexually abused only once in early childhood. Traumatic though the event may have been at the time, it is likely to have been buried emotionally. However, the demonic entities which came in through the incident have not forgotten, so when the girl grows up the demons do all they can to interfere with the sexual relationship in her marriage.

Adults abused in childhood often have gender confusion, promiscuity, prostitution, homosexuality, lesbianism and all sorts of sexual perversions. Often they become pedophiles themselves. Unless these demons are renounced and cast out they can cause a lifetime of misery.

Circumstances

A child is dependent upon the parent; completely at first, then less as he or she matures but at times circumstances may occur that are out of the parent's control. It might not seem fair or right that children can do things that allow demonizing, or that things can happen to them against their will that allow it, but there isn't anything Satan does that is fair or right. It serves to show us the awfulness of sin.

The Bible does say that very young children can be demonized. Mark 9:14-29 tells about a young boy who "from childhood" was possessed by a spirit that robbed him of speech, seized him and threw him to the ground. It made him foam at the mouth, gnash his teeth and become rigid. Mark 7:24-30 tells about a "little daughter" who was possessed by an evil spirit. These attacks can come from spirits who desire to act out ungodly deeds and acts. They often cause poverty, anger, poor health, rejection, rebellion and various types of psychoses. Unless they are commanded to leave in the name of Jesus, these spirits will remain with the child who can develop into an adult with many problems. The child has little control over family circumstances and poor protection by the parent at this weak and vulnerable time in life.

Temper Tantrums

As parents who are protecting our children, we must never allow them to get away with sinning. Remember that we must live a holy and godly life before them. That means that parents must control themselves and not display angry outbursts in the home.

We must never speak curses in the family home and never allow our child to curse us.

"*Whoso curseth his father or his mother, his lamp shall be put out in obscure darkness*" (Proverbs 20:20).

And, we must never allow our child to go into a temper tantrum. During a tantrum, a child has lost control of his spirit and is in a very dangerous and unprotected condition.

"He that hath no rule over his own spirit is like a city that is broken down, and without walls" (Proverbs 25:28).

Faith of the Parents

Deliverance for a child hinges upon the faith of the parent. In Matthew 15:22 a woman of Canaan brought her daughter to Jesus for deliverance. The mother knew exactly what was wrong with her daughter. She did not mince words; she said her daughter was grievously vexed with a devil. In Matthew 17:14-21 a man brought his son for deliverance (not for psychoanalysis) and Jesus cured him by casting out a devil. Even infants can be in need of deliverance and they can be quietly delivered while they sleep. However, children need the faith of their parents to not only get free, but to stay free.

Keeping the Child Delivered

After deliverance, the parents must keep their children delivered by consistently training and disciplining them. Although it may seem unfair, infants and children are subject to demonic attack. It lets one know the awesome responsibility of being a parent. Our actions can affect a multitude of descendants (Numbers 14:18; Exodus 20:5). Just as in the deliverance of an adult, the five-step procedure should be followed for children as well closing the doors to the devil.

Ministering to the Irrational

Insanity and madness are a part of the curse of the law (Deuteronomy 28:28). Madness comes upon a person when an insanity demon takes control of their mind (John 10:20). Once we discern that the insane condition is caused by a demon, we know there is a remedy according to God's Word (Mark 16:17).

There are, of course, instances where the mental problem comes from physical brain damage, etc., and in these cases there is another kind of remedy according to God's Word. There is need of physical healing and a restorative miracle. Medication may also be needed to bring the person back to a rational state. We are to be cognizant of the fact that at times we must refer people to mental health professionals. Always seek the wisdom of the Holy Spirit and never try to handle an out of control situation alone.

God wants us free! In studying Galatians 3:10-14 we see that God is telling us that Jesus made provision for us to be free from the curse of the law, and that we are not under the curse unless we place ourselves under the law. He tells us in verse 11 that the key to being free is to live by faith. How do we get to this place in faith? Read Romans 10:17 and Jude 20.

What Did Jesus Do?

Jesus is our Teacher. He dealt with the insane many

times in Scripture. A classic example is found in Mark 5:1-19. The man in Gadera was insane by reason of unclean spirits. In verse 6 the man's spirit was temporarily in control and he came willingly to Jesus and worshipped Him. In verse 7 the demons were in control and came against Jesus.

Jesus insisted the demons identify themselves in this instance while in other cases He did not. Jesus proceeded to cast the spirits out and then the man was in his right mind and got dressed. It is interesting to note that when he got delivered from the demons, he put on his clothes! That should tell us something about the condition of those who display public nudity and partial nudity wearing provocative and revealing clothing.

In Mark 5:19, Jesus told the man he had just delivered,

"Go home to thy friends and tell them how great things the Lord hath done for thee and hath had compassion on thee. And he departed, and began to publish in Decapolis how great things Jesus had done for him and all men did marvel."

Note that in Mark 9:38-40, John said,

"Master, we saw one casting out devils in thy name, and he followeth not us: and we forbad him, because he followeth not us. But Jesus said forbid him not for there is no man which shall do a miracle in my name that can lightly speak evil of me. For he that is not against us is on our part."

Is this perhaps the same man Jesus delivered who was previously called the demoniac of Gadera?

Jesus Quoted Scripture

It is only by using God's Word in the Name of Jesus that we have authority over demon powers (Mark 16:17). Jesus overcame the devil by quoting Scripture (Matthew 4) and so can we. Hebrews 3:1 shows that Jesus intercedes to the Father with words.

"Wherefore, holy brethren, partakers of the heavenly calling, consider the Apostle and High Priest of our profession, Christ Jesus."

It is important to understand that insanity (and other forms of demonic harassment and torment) often comes in waves. The tormented one should be prayed through these difficult times. The counselor will need to have the love and the mercy of God, and the patience of Job to see the extremely tormented person through to freedom.

If the person who is being prayed for is under the care of physicians, and on psychotropic medications, it is wise to ascertain whether or not they have taken the prescribed amount and not overdosed themselves in which case they would need immediate medical attention.

Teams of believers on shifts may be necessary during these "waves." Quote the Word, pray in the Spirit, praise the Lord, and plead the Blood of Jesus. Pleading the Blood of Jesus is like pleading a case in a court of law.

The Bible teaches us that when the enemy comes in like

a flood, the Lord will raise up the resistance against him (Isaiah 59:19). Although medications may be advisable at times to bring the person to a lucid enough state to fight a spiritual battle, it won't be injections, pills, or shock treatments that will ultimately set the demonized person free; it will be the Blood of Jesus and the Word of God!

When the demonic wave has subsided, continue to teach God's Word and encourage the person to resist the devil (James 4:7). Teach the person that these waves will get weaker and less frequent as the growth in the Lord progresses. Answer any and all rambling questions or statements by quoting an appropriate Scripture. Jesus often said, "Satan, it is written..."

Scripture is Our Weapon of War

In ministering to the irrational person, continually bombard his or her spirit with the Word of God. It is sharper than a two-edged sword and it penetrates the spirit (Hebrews 4:12, 13). Lead the person through the Scriptures. If there are no rational periods, saturate him or her with Scripture reading Ephesians 4:2, 3; 5:26 and Romans 12:2 to them. The mind will begin to be renewed and the Word will wash confusion away so that the person can call upon the Lord and be saved and set free.

Help the victim to realize that in the future, he or she must build faith with Scripture. The Word of God is the weapon that will set the individual free (Proverbs 4:20-22; John 8:31, 32). As the person begins to communicate, begin to search out how the door that gave the devil a legal right to attack the person, was opened in the first place.

By Little and Little

Remember, the Lord will drive out the enemy, as a person is able to hold his or her ground.

"By little and little I will drive them out from before thee, until thou be increased and inherit the land" (Exodus 23:24-33).

A person does not get taken over in a day so getting rid of a serious condition may take time as well. To be emptied out too quickly could bring back a worse condition. The individual also needs to be serious about filling his or her house with the Holy Spirit and the Word of God so as to hold the ground taken back from the demons (Matthew 12:43-45).

The Interview

The Initial Interview

Always begin the interview with prayer asking the Holy Spirit to be present and to give the discernment necessary to know how to minister to the one being counseled. Claim verbally the protection of the Blood of Jesus, bind the powers of darkness, anoint everyone present with oil and command the devil and his unclean spirits to stand at attention.

Allow the one coming for ministry to explain the specific problems and the type of manifestations he or she is experiencing. Ask why he or she feels there is a deliverance need to determine whether they are having trouble with demons, their flesh, or as is usually the case, both. Explore the counselee's spiritual condition. Is the person saved and baptized in the Holy Spirit? Explain the importance of being one of God's children and that if they are not, God is not obligated to deliver. Minister first to any salvation or Holy Spirit Baptism needs.

Begin to explain the reason for questioning them. Explain the legal transaction of renouncing the lie and confessing God's Word, the Truth. Explain, also, how they must take back the ground given to Satan and break his lease. Stress the importance of living a holy life before the Lord. Be sure there is complete sincerity in his or her Christian walk and there is willingness to meet the conditions necessary to accomplish deliverance and continued freedom.

Ask questions that will determine if ground has been given to the devil by words. For example, wrong confessions, and or nicknames. Curses brought on by the person and by others can have powerful effects. Explore the condition of their thoughts, their mind and imaginations. Are the meditations of the heart acceptable to God? Find out if ground has been given by acts of the body.

Taking Notes in the Interview

While counseling, prepare notes of ground to be taken back, curses to be broken and unclean sprits to be dealt with. The Holy Spirit will lead the process. Listen for areas where doors may have been opened to demons and where curses could have originated in the person's life. Since most demonic problems begin with the circumstances, abuses and traumas in childhood inquiries should include:

- Conditions in the childhood home. Was there abuse or trauma of any kind?

- After the counseling and note taking the counselee is ready for the actual ministry of deliverance.

- Depending upon how long and arduous the questioning is, another appointment may be necessary to complete the process.

Ministering Deliverance

The prayer room is like a court of law. Always have two or three Holy Spirit baptized believers ministering. The Bible says,

"In the mouths of two or three witnesses is a matter established" (Deuteronomy 19:15; 2 Corinthians 13:1; Matthew 18:16).

The devil is a legal expert -witnesses make it legal. Have a second person help with note taking and also with the actual ministry. If notes are compared, a more complete deliverance will be possible. Organize areas to renounce or take back and make notes of Scriptures to claim and spirits to come against. Pray over these notes, stirring up the gift of discerning of spirits so that what is being dealt with becomes clear.

Forgiveness

Contrary to popular belief, forgiveness is not an emotion; it is a decision, an act of the will. Neither is forgiveness forgetting. People who try to forgive by forgetting offenses suffered usually fail on both counts. It is possible to forgive without forgetting (Anderson 202). We must will to forgive those who have hurt us. It is good to make a list of everyone we need to forgive, go down the list and forgive each specific wrong, rejection, abuse, unfairness, betrayal, etc. Forgiveness is not so much for the persons we are forgiving as it is for our healing and deliverance. Being willing to forgive is leaving the justice up to God and getting set free.

Casting out the Devils

The prime purpose of renouncing or "taking back" is to facilitate the deliverance by removing the invitation to the devil and then replacing the affected area with the truth of God's Word. This takes back the legal right of demons and curses present (2 Timothy 2:25, 26; 2 Corinthians 4:2). When the legal right is gone, the demons have no footing and cannot put on a show of violent, silly, or talkative manifestations. Remember, *we are not to traffic (converse) with demons.*

Take back the legal right of each demon by looking up a Scripture that counters the sin referring to your Scripture index. Have the counselee read each Scripture aloud. This is how Jesus did it, by telling the devil, "It is written…" (Matthew 4:4).

Once all the groundwork is completed, cast the demons out taking authority over any manifestations which will usually be at a minimum once authority is taken. It is the Christian who is in charge. Some manifestations, however, are necessary as the spirits leave. These may include strange guttural sounds, coughing and or spitting, yawning, belching or burping.

Taking some deep breaths and exhaling will often assist the deliverance. Go down the list, item by item, helping the person to renounce the entry and claiming a Scripture that counters the manifestation. Do this a section at a time and then cast the spirits out one by one. Have the person verbally bind the spirit and command it to go. The counselee must:

- Forgive, by name, any involved person, living or dead and pray blessings upon them or their memory in order to break any curse (Judges 17:2; Luke 6:28).

- Pray and break any hereditary curses, forgiving relatives and ancestors and blessing them and or their memories.

- Cast the spirits out one by one.

- As a final gesture, have the individual tear up the notes. This helps them to know that the devil has lost his hold on them and that the session will remain confidential.

Instruct the counselee to not hold back any urges to cough, scream, belch, cry, etc., as holding back could hinder the deliverance. Upon completion of the deliverance session, lead the individual through these Blood Promises and instruct them on the advisability of memorizing them.

THE BLOOD PROMISES

My sins are forgiven by the Blood of Jesus.
I am redeemed by the Blood of Jesus, out of Satan's hand
I am justified and made righteous by the Blood of Jesus.
The Blood of Jesus protects me from all evil.
I belong to Jesus Christ, God's Son, spirit, soul and body.
Because of the Blood of Jesus,
Satan has no more power over me
No more place in me.
Jesus said, "These signs shall follow them that believe,
In My Name they shall cast out devils."
I am a believer,
And in the Name of Jesus,
I command you devil to get out of my life!

Concerning Confidentiality

It is of vital importance that matters being discussed in the deliverance room be confidential if the individual prefers it that way. Many times situations may be discussed for training, educational or intercessory prayer purposes, but it is imperative that names of the individuals are never revealed.

Finding and Binding the Strongman

How Do We Bind The Strongman?

The Bible tells us that "No *man can enter into a strongman's house and spoil his goods; except he will first bind the strongman and then he will spoil his house"* (Mark 3:27).

In Ephesians 6:12 we are given the organizational chart, so to speak, the positions, names, and job titles of ruling spirits. They are principalities, powers, and the rulers of darkness of this world, and spiritual wickedness in high (heavenly) places. Just exactly who are these spirits and what do they do?

- PRINCIPALITIES are supervisory wicked spirits over a geographic area.

- POWERS are supervisory wicked spirits over a certain type of wickedness.

- RULERS OF DARKNESS are the many assistants assigned to individuals or assigned to harass groups of individuals, churches, etc.

We must bind these strongmen of the heavenlies. We

must cast out the strongmen and their assistants (unclean spirits). We must cast out these spirits who have been assigned to individuals and cancel their assignments.

Three Wicked Spirit Powers

Travis Walters, in his book entitled, He Laughs in the Heavens claims that the Lord gave him the revelation of the essence of the demonic kingdom as being an unholy trinity. "The Holy Trinity consists of the Father, the Son (Jesus), and the Holy Spirit but the unholy trinity consists of three wicked spirit powers who attempt to undo God's divine order. They are: 1) Antichrist, 2) Death and Hell and 3) Jezebel. There are other evil entities as well but these are the ones who cause the most trouble among Christians."

Walters goes on to say, "We must remember that Satan declared,

"I will make myself like the Most High" (Isaiah 14:14).

Almighty God is Three-in-One. The devil, through the unholy trinity, has attempted to become three-in-one as well, although he is incapable of doing so because he is a creature and is not omniscient, omnipotent nor is he omnipresent. Nevertheless, he has tried. The spirit of antichrist is the counterpart of God the Father, Death and Hell stands over against Jesus the Son, and Jezebel is the counterfeit of the Holy Spirit" (Walters 56-57).

In the Holy Trinity, all authority issues forth from God the Father. Therefore, the assignment of the spirit of antichrist is to pollute and destroy all godly authority in order to make way for the coming man of lawlessness (the antichrist), whose authority will be completely satanic. The work of the unholy trinity includes:

- War against God the Father and attempts to discredit Him and His children.

- War against Jesus the Son and attempts to block salvation, healing, deliverance, and our other God given provisions.

- War against the Holy Spirit and attempts to rob God's children of power.

Insight into the Work of these Three Wicked Spirit Powers

Antichrist: is a ruler in the heavenlies (1 John 4:1-6). His major responsibility is rebellion versus submission (Hebrews 13:17). He is in charge of the promotion of rebellion in those under authority and promotion of putting the wrong person in positions of authority. He is also in charge of encouraging the right person to refuse a position of authority.

Manifestations of Antichrist

The antichrist spirit is often in operation in those who are living a life that is not righteous and upright before the Lord, one who questions the need of authority and are of the opinion that one need not submit to anyone but Christ (Hebrews 13:17). Another manifestation of this spirit can be seen in those who are always striving to be number one in power and or prestige. The one seeking power may also seek out a Jezebel (witchcraft spirit) to help build his or her ungodly kingdom.

Death and Hell is also a ruler in the heavenlies (Revelation 20:13, 14). His major responsibilities are to stop evangelists from proclaiming the gospel and preventing people from getting saved by distractions and deceptions. He also manifests by attempting to prevent healings and miracles from taking place.

Manifestations of Death and Hell

Those under the influence of the death and hell spirit will often live in immorality and domination by the works of the flesh. They also often display extreme self-reliance. They may suffer from various physical infirmities, along with many types of fears, phobias and doubts which leave them discontented and restless. They are usually unaware of the supernatural realm.

Jezebel is also a ruler in the heavenlies. In Revelation 2:18-25 we see Jezebel as a spirit over churches. In Isaiah 47:1-15 she is portrayed as the daughter of Babylon (confusion). This portion of Scripture lists several curses linked to this spirit. The major responsibilities of this spirit are to minimize the male influence in authority and to dominate by radical feminist authority. Prophetic ministries are destroyed by keeping people from becoming doers of God's Word.

Manifestations of Jezebel

The Jezebel spirit hates the prophetic ministry and those under the influence of this spirit seek to silence God's prophets. In so doing it destroys the testimony of Jesus, the spirit of prophesy (Revelation 19:10). Jezebel is a religious spirit that counterfeits the gifts of the Spirit working witchcraft, manipulation, immorality, seduction, lust, perversion and lasciviousness. The influence of this spirit often causes individuals to take sin very lightly.

The desire to delve into the occult and the deep things of Satan are prevalent in the victims of this spirit. They also may come from families with patterns of divorce, having sons who are female in their emotions and daughters who are male in theirs resulting in addictions, drug abuse and miscellaneous mental problems.

How Does This Relate To Deliverance?

Satan's domain is extremely organized, and so, we must also be organized if we expect to be victorious over him. Experience has shown that in our actual systematic ministering of deliverance, it is very helpful to first bind the strongman. Then bind the powers in the heavenlies controlling the strongman. Verbally, and with hand gestures, cut the cords of control over the subordinates within the individual, the family or the body of believers if there is trouble in the Church.

Secondly, we should cast out the strongman subordinates. Then, we can proceed with renouncing and casting out of spirits identified during the counseling of the individual.

Important Keys to Staying Free

Consistency — The Key to Staying Free

After surgery, a patient receives a list of things they should and should not do. In just the same way, after deliverance there are things we can do to ensure that people grow strong again and able to withstand the many ongoing attacks of the evil one. Satan does not give a person up easily and will try to reclaim the ground that he has lost. The following guidelines will be helpful to people who are determined to walk in obedience to the Lord Jesus Christ.

- Jesus is Lord and should be priority number one in the person's life, not just at the new birth experience but continuously.

- Holy Spirit filling should be in the person's life, not just the initial baptism of the Holy Spirit but consistently.

- Read the Word daily and consistently because the Scripture contains everything we need for Godly living.

- The armor of God is for our defense and protection. Study Ephesians 6:10-18 so that we will be able to stand against the attacks of the enemy consistently.

- Fellowship consistently with other Christian believers and have a body of believers around, not old friends.

- Forgiveness, godliness, holiness, and love should be walked in consistently.

- Praise God consistently for who He is and what He has done.

- Thankful and grateful should be the attitude of the heart toward God for everything, and in everything, consistently.

Replacement

Since our minds are created to entertain only one thought at a time, it is possible to displace the enemy's tormenting, obsessive thoughts with God's thoughts (Scripture). Gradually the torment will ease as verses from God's Word replace the wrong thoughts. If the counselee stumbles and falls, or continues to be tormented again after deliverance, it does not necessarily mean that he or she has lost the ground that has been gained. These thoughts have been placed in the mind by the devil. We must not be fooled. The devil is a liar and the father of them (John 8:44).

If a person's mind has been trained to dwell on fantasies, or on some other lies of the devil, he or she may need to recite Scriptures like the following every time those thoughts come:

For though we walk in the flesh, we do not war after the flesh: For the weapons of our warfare are not carnal, but mighty through God to the pulling down of strongholds; casting down imaginations and every high thing that exalteth itself against the knowledge of God, and bringing into captivity every thought to the obedience of Christ (2 Corinthians 10:3-5).

Satan's thoughts are like arrows that have been shot at the mind. Scripture acts like a brick wall, stopping the arrows, protecting and guarding the mind against the attack. Eventually victory will come. Deliverance has been established in the mouth of two or three witnesses (2 Corinthians 13:1). God's Word is settled in heaven forever (Psalms 119:89).

Called to Minister Deliverance

We are called to minister deliverance as Jesus did. Both the authority and the freedom He promises lie in intimacy with Him.

"The Spirit of the Lord is upon me, because he hath anointed me to preach the gospel to the poor; he hath sent me to heal the brokenhearted, to preach deliverance to the captives, and recovering of sight to the blind, to set at liberty them that are bruised, to preach the acceptable year of the Lord" (Luke 4:18, 19).

Here Jesus gives the purpose of His Spirit-anointed ministry. It is to preach the gospel to the poor, the destitute, the afflicted, the humble, those crushed in spirit, the brokenhearted, and those who tremble at His Word. His Spirit anointed ministry is to heal those who are bruised and oppressed. This healing involves the total person, both physical and spiritual. It is to open the spiritual eyes of those blinded by the world and Satan in order that they might see the truth of God's good news. It is to proclaim the time of true freedom and salvation from Satan's domain, sin, fear, and guilt.

All those who are filled with the Holy Spirit are called to share in Jesus' ministry in these ways. To do so we must gain a deep realization of the terrible need and misery of the human race that has resulted from sin and the power of Satan – a condition of enslavement to evil, broken heartedness, bondage, spiritual blindness, and physical distress. Jesus' foremost concern during His earthly ministry was to destroy the works of the devil (I John 3:8). There can be no realization of the kingdom of God without confronting the kingdom of Satan.

In Conclusion

This book is by no means meant to be an exhaustive listing of demons or a complete teaching on spiritual warfare. Nor is it meant to be the last word on spiritual warfare. Rather, it is a book of general principles regarding that warfare. It is an illustration of a method of deliverance that works. The Scriptures are clear, Jesus was clear... demons are real, they are a menace to mankind and they need to be dealt with for Christians to be able to walk in victory. Of course, God can deliver us from demonic powers any way He wants to, He is not limited to this method. It is but one of many. Hopefully you will search the Scriptures and find for yourself that demonic oppression is real, but so is deliverance.

The signs are all around us making it obvious that we are living in the last days of the end times. Sin is abounding in the world and we will be engaged in spiritual warfare more than ever from now until the Lord's return. Carnal weapons such as human talent, wealth, ability, charisma and personality are in themselves insufficient to pull down the strongholds of the devil. The only weapons powerful enough to destroy the fortresses of Satan are those that God gives. These weapons are powerful because they are spiritual. The weapons He gives us are the weapons of faith, a life of righteousness and holiness, a commitment to truth, to proclaiming the gospel, the hope of salvation, and the power of the Holy Spirit. Learning how to effectively use these weapons of warfare is crucial. It is time for Christians to stop their defensive rationalizing, justifying, and explaining away their sin and begin to learn how to combat the enemy. Ignoring the devil is not an option and will not cause him to simply go away.

In these last days we need to focus our minds on Christ and heavenly things rather than on earthly things more than ever before and in these last days we will also be tempted as never before to focus instead on the world. If we want to live in victory and peace we must set our minds on the Spirit of God.

"For the mind set on the Spirit is life and peace" (Romans 8-6-7).

Although the deliverance ministry has faded into oblivion over the last few decades there is evidence that in recent years there has been a re-emergence and validating of the deliverance ministry that was so prevalent in the 1960's and 1970's "Jesus Movement." Therefore, we see the necessity for training Christians as deliverance counselors to understand the inner workings of demons and to be able to see themselves and their brothers and sisters in Christ set free. This book was written for this purpose, to teach Christians how to use the weapons of our warfare effectively and to teach them that combating demonic oppression is necessary for the physical, spiritual, psychological, and emotional growth of the Christian in the 21st Century.

Works Cited

Anderson, Neil T. "<u>Victory Over The Darkness: Realizing the Power of Your Identity In Christ.</u>" Regal Books, A Division of Gospel Light, Ventura, CA., 1990: 202.

Anderson, Neil T. and Steve Russo. "<u>The Seduction of Our Children: Protecting Kids From Satanism, New Age and The Occult.</u>" Harvest House Publishers Eugene, OR 1991: 33, 230.

Ankerberg, John and John Weldon. "<u>The Facts on the New Age Movement: Answers to the 30 Most Frequently Asked Questions About the New Age Movement.</u>" Harvest House Publishers Eugene, OR 1988: 7.

Carlton, Del. "<u>Outright Warfare</u>" Morris Publishing, Kearney NE.

Garrison, Mary. "<u>How To Conduct Spiritual Warfare As I See It</u>!" Garrison, Hudson, FL. 1980: 29.

Holy Bible, Living Translation

Holy Bible, King James Version

Horrobin, Peter J. "<u>Healing through Deliverance</u>." Chosen Books Division of Baker Book House, Grand Rapids, MI. 1991, 2003: 13, 56.

Hunt, Dave. "The Cult Explosions: An Exposes of Today's Cults and Why They Prosper." Harvest House Publishers Eugene, OR 1980: 240.

Ingram, Chip. "The Invisible War: What Every Believer Needs to Know About Satan, Demons, and Spiritual Warfare." Baker Books, Grand Rapids, MI. 2006: 129.

Koch, Kurt. "Christian Counselling and Occultism: An Investigation Covering Medicine, Psychiatry, Psychology, Depth-Psychology, Religious-Psychology, Parapsychology and Theology." Kregel Publications, Division of Kregel, Inc. Grand Rapids, MI. 1978: 249.

"New World Dictionary of American English," Third College Edition. Simon & Shuster, Inc. New York, NY, 1988

Otis, George K. II. "Like a Roaring Lion." Time Light Division of Bible Voice, Van Nuys, CA. 1973.

Prince, Derek. "They Shall Expel Demons: What You Need To Know About Demons – Your Invisible Enemies." Chosen Books division of Baker Book House, Grand Rapids, MI. 1998: 89.

Reisser, Paul C., MD, Teri Reisser, and John Weldon. "New Age Medicine: A Christian Perspective on Holistic Health." Inter Varsity Press, Downers Grove, IL 1987: 148-151.

Thompson, Carroll. "The Bruises of Satan." Carroll Thompson Ministries, Inc. Dallas, TX 1992: 19.

Walters, Travis. "He Laughs in the Heavens: A Songbook for End-Time Warriors." Travis Walters 1978: 56-57

Weber, Stu. "Spirit Warriors: Strategies for the Battles Christian Men and Women Face Every Day." Multnomah Publishers, Inc. Sisters, OR 2001: 162.

CPSIA information can be obtained at www.ICGtesting.com
Printed in the USA
LVOW082212281012

304783LV00001B/5/P